S

GW00597779

Bay of Biscay

FRANCE

SPAIN

PORTUGAL

● Madrid

SEVILLE ●

Mediterranean Sea

MOROCCO   ALGERIA

HarperCollins*Publishers*

This book was produced using QuarkXPress™ and
Adobe Illustrator 88™ on Apple Macintosh™ computers
and output to separated film on a Linotronic™ 300 Imagesetter

Text: Hilary Macartney with additional contributions by
George Kean
Photography: Douglas Robertson
Cartography: Susan Harvey Design
Design: Lynsey Roxburgh

First published 1991
Copyright © HarperCollins Publishers
Published by HarperCollins Publishers
Printed in Hong Kong
ISBN 0 00 435795 7

HOW TO USE THIS BOOK

Your Collins Traveller Guide will help you find your way around your holiday destination quickly and easily. It is split into two sections which are colour-coded:

The blue section provides you with an alphabetical sequence of headings, from **BUILDINGS** to **WALKS** via **EXCURSIONS**, **MUSEUMS**, **RESTAURANTS**, etc. Each entry within a topic includes information on how to get there, how much it will cost you, when it will be open and what to expect. Furthermore, every page has its own map showing the position of each item and the nearest landmark. This allows you to orientate yourself quickly and easily in your new surroundings. To find what you want to do – having dinner, visiting a museum, going for a walk or sightseeing – simply flick through the blue headings and take your pick!

The red section is an alphabetical list of information. It provides essential facts about places and cultural items – 'What are *rejas*?', 'When is Semana Santa?', 'Where is the Palacio de San Telmo?' – and expands on subjects touched on in the first half of the book. This section also contains practical travel information. It ranges through how to find accommodation, information on driving, the variety of eating places and food available, tips on health, information on money, which newspapers are available, how to use the telephone system and where to find water-sports facilities. It is lively and informative and easy to use. Each band shows the first three letters of the first entry on the page. Simply flick through the bands till you find the entry you need!

All the main entries are also cross-referenced to help you find them. Names in small capitals – **MUSEUMS** – tell you that there is more information about the item you are looking for under the topic on museums in the first part of the book. So when you read 'see **MUSEUMS**' you turn to the blue heading for **MUSEUMS**. The instruction 'see **A-Z**' after a word, lets you know that the word has its own entry in the second part of the book. Similarly words in bold type – **Ceramics** – also let you know that there is an entry in the A-Z for the indicated name. In both cases you just look under the appropriate heading in the red section.

Packed full of information and easy to use – you'll always know where you are with your Collins Traveller Guide.

INTRODUCTION

Seville has been attracting tourists ever since the 19thC Romantics fell in love with the city. Today 'Sevilla' (pronounced 'sebee-lya') is a bustling modern city of around 700,000 inhabitants, Spain's fourth largest city and capital of the autonomous region of Andalucía, but its rich mixture of Moorish and European architecture, its fragrant orange-tree walks and its lively and colourful traditions remain. In short, its power to enchant and delight is as strong as ever.

Myth and fact have become interwoven in Seville's history. A good example is the popular saying: 'Hercules built me; Caesar surrounded me with walls and towers; the King Saint took me.' Hercules of course belongs to mythology and there is little evidence that Julius Caesar did begin building the city walls in 45 BC. In 1248, however, the city was indeed reconquered for Christianity by King Ferdinand III, later St. Ferdinand or San Fernando, thus ending more than five centuries of Islam and Moorish rule. Between the Roman and Moorish civilizations the city was occupied by the Vandals in the 5thC, followed by the Visigoths during the 5th-8thC, when Seville became an important centre of Christianity.

The Moors erected their buildings upon those of Romans and Visigoths, and the Christians who followed them likewise built on Moorish sites, for example at the Reales Alcázares, where the fantasy palace of King Pedro the Cruel was built on the site of the earlier Moorish palace and incorporated elements of it. Similarly, the huge Gothic Cathedral was built on the site of the grand mosque. Many of the buildings of the new Christian era, such as King Pedro's palace, continued to display the remarkable talents of *mudéjar* (Muslim) craftsmen in decorative stucco, ceramics, wood and brickwork. Even the Cathedral, otherwise thoroughly European in style, retained the beautiful Moorish Giralda tower, once the most admired minaret of the Muslim world, as its bell tower.

With the capture of the Moors' last stronghold at Granada in 1492, the Christian Reconquest of Spain was complete. In the same year, Christopher Columbus discovered America and claimed it for the Spanish Crown. These events ushered in Spain's Golden Age of the

16th-17thC in which Seville's role, both economically and artistically, was of enormous importance. The port city gained the monopoly on all Spanish trade with the Indies: an unprecedented wealth of gold and silver was unloaded at the docks, precious stones and metals were traded on the steps of the Cathedral and Seville became renowned as the world's richest city. As the 16thC progressed, an impressive Lonja or trade exchange was built and other grand buildings such as the Ayuntamiento (Town Hall) reflected the city's new civic pride. Aristocrats and rich merchants also displayed their wealth and taste in superb houses such as the Casa de Pilatos. In the 17thC, Seville produced some of Spain's most important artists, among them Velázquez and Murillo. By the end of that century, its importance as a port was declining but its links with the Indies continued with the construction of the massive new Fábrica de Tabacos (now the University) in the 18thC and

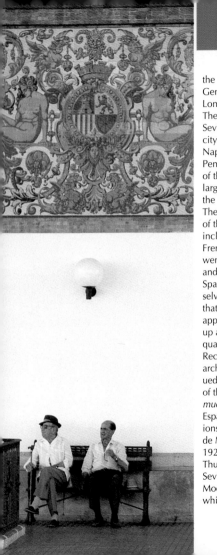

the creation of the Archivo General de las Indias within the Lonja building.

The 19thC saw the 'discovery' of Seville by the Romantics. The city was occupied by Napoleon's troops during the Peninsular War at the beginning of that century and there was large-scale looting of art from the churches and convents. These events drew the attention of the rest of Europe and writers including Lord Byron and the Frenchman Théophile Gautier went to sample Seville's delights and publish its attractions. Spaniards and Sevillians themselves increasingly recognized that their city had a unique appeal and set about cleaning up and preserving the old Jewish quarter. Tourism had arrived! Recognition of Seville's special architectural heritage has continued this century with the revival of the *mudéjar* style as *neo-mudéjar*, notably in the Pl. de España and some of the pavilions in and around the Parque de María Luisa erected for the 1929 Ibero-American Exhibition. Thus the present-day visitor to Seville is surrounded by a Moorish-inspired tradition which spans the 12th-20thC.

The Universal Exhibition in Seville in 1992, Expo '92, has provided a further opportunity for a rich new architectural mix: modern hi-tech pavilions with the very latest in climatic control surround the restored Carthusian monastery which once housed the remains of Columbus with, alongside, the chimneys of the famous La Cartuja ceramics factory, all of them now united by the theme of 'The Age of Discovery'. Seville is synonymous with fiestas. Few places have more, both sacred and profane. During the world-famous Semana Santa (Holy Week) celebrations, religion takes to the streets: sinister, hooded penitents accompany the slow processions of spectacularly decked out and bejewelled images of the Virgin or tortured sculptures of the crucified Christ, backed up by brass bands playing sombre marches. Women beat their breasts and cry out and occasionally a heart-rending lament, a *saeta*, pierces the air and reduces everyone to silence. In little more than a week, the city and its citizens undergo a complete change of mood in time to celebrate the Feria de Abril (April Fair). The penitent's robes are exchanged for the caballero's waistcoat, cropped trousers and sombrero in the horseback processions, while women wear bright dresses, all flounces and frills, familiar to us from postcards. Night after night is spent eating and drinking and dancing the ever-popular *sevillanas*, with the revellers frequently not returning home till morning. But Seville doesn't just come alive for special celebrations. The climate and a naturally gregarious people mean that much of life is lived on the streets. In the evenings after work, groups of people gather outside bars for a drink and the inevitable snack of *tapas*; tourists and Sevillians mix in the crowded open-air bars and restaurants of the Barrio de Santa Cruz and the *terrazas* along the river in Triana and, later, the streets around the late-night bars and discos of Los Remedios literally throng with young people. A favourite Sevillian pastime is to dress up and go for a stroll to see and be seen. Along c/ Sierpes and around the Cathedral, window-shopping and people-watching become a positive ritual on Saturdays after the siesta and on Sundays before lunch. Walking is by far the best way of getting to know Seville, though a ride in a horse-drawn carriage can be both a romantic treat and a good way of getting to know the general layout of the city, while a boat trip gives an even wider perspective. Seville is also an ideal base for excursions

and tours. Nearby are the Roman sites at Itálica and Carmona, and Córdoba, capital of Moorish Andalucía, with its incomparable mosque. Jerez has sherry-sampling at bodegas and there are many spectacular hill towns to explore, as well as the Coto de Doñana Nature Reserve.

Expo '92 has focused the world's attention once more on Seville. Buildings have been restored and communications and transport vastly improved. Within Spain, Seville used to be regarded as the backward, if picturesque, southern cousin of Barcelona and Madrid and a Sevillian accent was often laughed at. Now the *sevillanas* are a dance craze among young people throughout Spain and many of the city's artists, fashion designers and pop musicians have achieved international success in recent years. Seville's new image is modern and sophisticated. Nevertheless, it is the romantic image of Seville which remains the strongest attraction for foreign visitors and the exotic aspects of the city, such as the distinctly non-European elements of its architecture, continue to fascinate. Like the 19thC Romantics, present-day visitors to Seville seek an assurance that Europe is not yet entirely bland and rational. The city's colourful pomp, the unbridled passion of flamenco and gypsy song and dance, and even the contentious ritual of the bullfight provide that assurance. Not surprisingly, Seville has provided the backdrop for several operas, from Bizet's *Carmen* to Rossini's *The Barber of Seville*. The myths of Don Juan and Carmen both originated in the city. Both were treacherous in love, yet are universally fascinating.

Seville is a city not to be missed. As the proverb says, 'Quien no ha visto a Sevilla, no ha visto a maravilla' – If you haven't seen Seville, you've missed a marvel!

Plaza de España

CATEDRAL Pl. Virgen de los Reyes.
❑ 1100-1700 Mon.-Fri., 1100-1600 Sat., 1400-1600 Sun. ❑ 225ptas.
The world's largest Gothic cathedral, rich in paintings, sculpture and silver, with a spectacular altarpiece plus the tomb of Columbus. See **A-Z***.*

GIRALDA Pl. Virgen de los Reyes.
❑ 1100-1700 Mon.-Fri., 1100-1600 Sat. & Sun. ❑ Included in Catedral price; 100ptas when Catedral closed.
The best-known symbol of Seville. 12thC minaret converted into cathedral bell tower rising 97 m. Incomparable views from the top. See **A-Z***.*

REALES ALCÁZARES Pl. del Triunfo.
❑ 1030-1800 Tue.-Sat., 1000-1400 Sun. ❑ General visit 250ptas.
Fortified Moorish palace rebuilt by Christian kings in mudéjar *style. Beautiful stuccowork and tiling, patios and gardens. See* **Alcázares***.*

LONJA Av de la Constitución.
❑ 1000-1300 Mon.-Sat. ❑ Free.
16thC trade exchange by Herrera in severe classical style. See **MUSEUMS***.*

CASA DE PILATOS Pl. de Pilatos.
❑ 0900-1800. ❑ Ground floor 200ptas; upper floor 200ptas.
Seville's finest 16thC house – mudéjar and Renaissance, with antique *sculptures, important tilework and a stunning cupola. See* **Pilatos***.*

HOSPITAL DE LA CARIDAD c/ Temprado.
❑ 1000-1300, 1530-1800 Mon.-Sat., 1030-1230 Sun. ❑ 100ptas.
17thC hospital of charity built for Miguel de Mañara. See **Caridad***.*

TORRE DEL ORO Paseo de Cristóbal Colón.
❑ 1000-1400 Tue.-Sat., 1000-1300 Sun. ❑ 150ptas.
Another of Seville's best-loved symbols. See **MUSEUMS***,* **A-Z***.*

AYUNTAMIENTO Pl. Nueva.
❑ Enquire 1000-1300 for visits to council chamber. ❑ Free.
16thC Plateresque Town Hall. View from Pl. de San Francisco. See **A-Z***.*

FÁBRICA DE TABACOS c/ San Fernando.
❑ Access to public areas, usually 0800-2000. ❑ Free.
Spain's second-largest building, built in the 18thC. Once Carmen's tobacco factory; now the main building of Seville University. See **A-Z**.

PLAZA DE ESPAÑA Av de Isabel la Católica.
❑ Limited access to public areas of interior 1000-1300. ❑ Free.
The centrepiece of the 1929 Ibero-American Exhibition. An impressive semicircular building overlooking a plaza with canal and ornamental bridges. See **España**.

HOSPICIO DE LOS VENERABLES Pl. de los Venerables.
❑ 1000-1400, 1600-2000 Mon.-Sat., 1000-1400 Sun. ❑ 200ptas.
Good example of Sevillian Baroque (see **A-Z**). *Attractive patio (see* **A-Z**) *and stairway; paintings by 17thC Seville artists. See* **Venerables**.

IGLESIA DE SAN SALVADOR Pl. Salvador.
❑ 1830-2100 Mon.-Sat., 1000-1330, 1830-2100 Sun. ❑ Free.
Seville's second 'cathedral' (17thC) has a notable Baroque (see **A-Z**) *altarpiece, as well as a much-revered carving of Christ, and the patio (see* **A-Z**) *of the original mosque.*

IGLESIA DE LA MAGDALENA Pl. de la Magdalena.
❑ Open before and after services. ❑ Free.
Beautiful example of Sevillian Baroque (see **A-Z**) *church architecture. Its cupola shows an inventive mix of* mudéjar *(see* **A-Z**) *and Aztec motifs.*

IGLESIA DE SANTA ANA Pl. de la Sacra Familia.
❑ 1830-2000. ❑ Free.
Triana's most important church combines Gothic (see **A-Z**) *and* mudéjar *(see* **A-Z**) *with later Renaissance elements. The interior has an impressive altarpiece, paintings and silver.*

CONVENTO DE LA CARTUJA Recinto de la Cartuja.
The 15thC monastery where Columbus was once buried. It has now been restored as the Royal Pavilion of Expo '92 (see **A-Z**). *See* **Cartuja**.

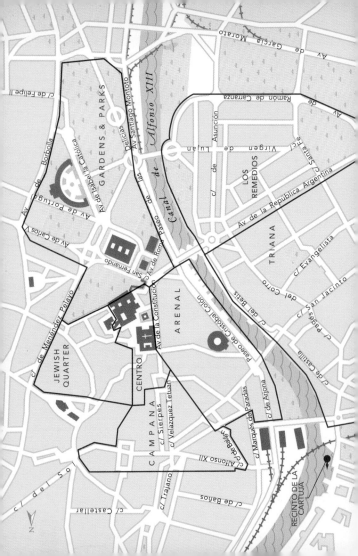

CENTRO
A fascinating architectural ensemble including the Reales Alcázares and austere Lonja, the massive Catedral and its Moorish Giralda tower. North is the Pl. Nueva and the Ayuntamiento. See BUILDINGS 1.

JEWISH QUARTER
The Barrio de Santa Cruz is a picturesque maze of narrow streets. Many bars, restaurants, crafts and souvenir shops. Further east is the Barrio de San Bartolomé and superb Casa de Pilatos. See BUILDINGS 1, WALKS 1 & 2.

CAMPANA
The main shopping area. The pedestrianized c/ Sierpes and nearby streets have smart shops. Large department stores including El Corte Inglés are in and around c/ Campana. See SHOPPING 1 & 2.

GARDENS & PARKS
Southeast of the centre, these include the Pl. de España and the extensive Parque de María Luisa with the museums on Pl. de América. See BUILDINGS 2, MUSEUMS, WALK 4.

ARENAL
Old port area of the city, with the Torre del Oro, Hospital de la Caridad, bullring and Iglesia de la Magdalena. See BUILDINGS 1 & 2, WALK 3.

RECINTO DE LA CARTUJA
The site of Expo '92 (see A-Z*) takes its name from the monastery restored as the Royal Pavilion, as does the 19thC ceramics factory which stands nearby. See* BUILDINGS 2, **Cartuja**.

TRIANA
A lively area which is good for traditional ceramics (see A-Z*), fish restaurants and splendid views across the river.*

LOS REMEDIOS
Also across the river, a sophisticated new area. Discos and late-night bars make it extremely popular with young people. See NIGHTLIFE 1 & 2.

Many of the artesanías (craft shops) continue to reflect the city's rich cultural heritage.

CERÁMICA SANTA ANA c/ San Jorge 31.
One of several shops still producing and selling Triana's traditional painted earthenware. It is worth a visit for its decorated exterior alone. See **Ceramics**.

TRIANA c/ de la Pureza 66.
High-quality silver- and goldsmithing continues a craft associated with Seville's Moorish and Jewish past and its trade with the Indies.

BORDADOS ARTESANÍA Pl. Doña Elvira.
Embroidered textiles, including the shawls and mantillas worn with sevillanas (see **A-Z**) *costume; also modern tapestries. See* **WALK 1**.

FORJA HISPALENSE c/ de la Feria 130.
Specializes in decorative wrought ironwork, another legacy of Andalucía's Moorish past.

GUARNICIONERÍA SAN PABLO c/ de Bailén s/n.
Tiny Andalusian-style saddlery which also sells other handmade leather items.

HERMANOS RAMÍREZ c/ Purgatorio 6.
Specializes in castanets (castañuelas or palillos) in traditional pomegranate wood (granadilla) or modern composites. Choose size 5 for older children, 6 and 7 for adults.

A PANTOJA c/ del Pozo 20.
A shop for guitar enthusiasts, with both classical and flamenco instruments in stock.

CASA RUBIO c/ Sierpes 56.
Famous shop specializing in traditional and modern Spanish fans (abanicos) – not just an accessory in the summer heat.

Itálica

2 hr 30 min round trip by car including visit and light refreshments; half a day by public transport. Buses leave from Estación de Autobuses, c/ M. V. Sagastizabal. Several companies, including Técnica GAT, operate excursion buses bookable at travel agents and at some hotels.

Take the N 630 (signposted Mérida) for 8 km to Santiponce. Restaurants in and around the town specialize in barbecued beef. Itálica is 1 km beyond to the northwest.

The first Roman (see **A-Z**) settlement on the Iberian Peninsula, Itálica was founded in 206 BC by Scipio Africanus after the Carthaginians had been routed at Carmona (see **EXCURSION 2**). It was elevated to colony status under Emperor Hadrian in the 2ndC AD. The first 'Spaniard' to become Roman Emperor was Trajan (AD 98-117), followed by Hadrian (AD 117-138). Both were born at Itálica which then probably occupied part of modern Santiponce. The ruins on the present site (0900-1730 Tue.-Sat., 1000-1600 Sun.; 250ptas) date from the 2ndC AD, the period of expansion commenced under Hadrian. The town flourished during the next two centuries and the vast amphitheatre, built for a capacity of 25,000, is evidence of its importance and splendour. In addition there are the remains of a forum, the theatre, baths and paved streets. Several villas have been excavated and important mosaics discovered. Itálica declined with the growing importance of Seville.

Over the centuries much has disappeared from the site, though it has not always been lost: the antique columns in c/ Mármoles (see **WALK 2**) and at the Alameda de Hércules (see **Hercules**) in Seville may have come from Itálica, while the mosaics at the Palacio de la Condesa de Lebrija (see **Lebrija**) certainly did. Now most of the important finds go to Seville's Museo Arqueológico (see **MUSEUMS**). There is a small museum on the site and, in summer, music and drama is sometimes performed in the amphitheatre.

Returning to Santiponce, the Monastery of San Isidoro del Campo is on the outskirts. Founded at the end of the 13thC by Alfonso Guzmán el Bueno, it has now been restored as a *parador* (see **A-Z**). It has two churches in Gothic (see **A-Z**) and *mudéjar* (see **A-Z**) style and a 17thC altarpiece and sculptures by Martínez Montañés. The Monastery was the first burial place of the conquistador, Hernán Cortés.

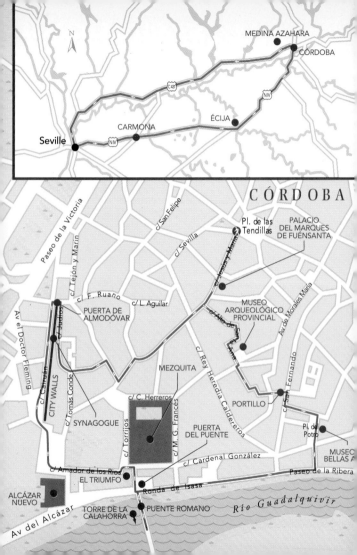

Carmona & Córdoba

A two-day round trip, including an overnight stay in Córdoba.

The route follows the N IV for the whole distance to Córdoba.

33 km – Carmona. Tourist information: Pl. de las Descalzas s/n. Carmona became part of the Roman Empire (see **Romans**) in 206 BC and was known as one of the most powerful cities in the Iberian Peninsula. On the approach to the town is the Roman Necropolis and Museum (0900-1400, 1600-1800 Tue.-Sat., 0900-1400 Sun.; 250ptas), with tombs dating mainly from the 1stC AD, including the grand Tomb of Servilia. The walled hill town is entered by the Puerta de Sevilla with its Moorish (see **A-Z**) arch and impressive Alcázar (1000-1400, 1600-1800 Tue.-Sat., 1000-1400 Sun.; 150ptas). Steep streets lead to Pl. San Fernando. Beyond are the imposing churches of San Salvador and 15thC Santa María. Other handsome buildings include Palacio de los Rueda, Palacio de los Aguilar and the *mudéjar* (see **A-Z**) Convent of Santa Clara. c/ San José leads to the Alcázar of Pedro the Cruel, now a *parador* (see **A-Z**), with commanding views over La Campina plain.

87 km – Écija. Tourist information: Av de Andalucía s/n. Eleven church towers can be counted on approaching the aptly nicknamed 'Town of Towers'. Among numerous churches and convents are 15thC Santiago, the Convent of Las Teresas in a 14thC *mudéjar* palace and the superb 18thC Convent of Los Descalzos. Around Pl. de España fine buildings include the Baroque (see **A-Z**) palaces of Peñaflor, Benamejí (which has a horse-drawn carriage collection) and Valdehermoso.

143 km – Córdoba. Tourist information: c/ Torrijos 10. The main square, Pl. de las Tendillas, has shops, banks and bars. The c/ Jesús y María leads south, past the 16thC Palacio del Marques de Fuénsanta, now the Conservatory of Music. Beyond, c/ Alto de Santa Ana leads to the Museo Arqueológico Provincial (1000-1400, 1700-2000 Tue.-Sat., 1000-1400 Sun.; 250ptas), where well-displayed exhibits lead the visitor through the city's development from Iberian settlement and Roman capital of the province of Baetica to its zenith as the capital of an independent Moorish caliphate (AD 929-1031) (see **Moors**). c/ Julio Romero Torres leads to the Portillo, an arched gateway which divided the west and east quarters of the city. Beyond c/ San Fernando, along c/ Romero Barro, is the fountain and Pl. del Potro (of the colt), with the Museo de

Mezquita

Bellas Artes (1000-1400, 1800-2000 Tue.-Sun.; 250ptas), housing a collection of Spanish paintings, and the Museo Julio Romero Torres (same times and prices), dedicated to the popular 20thC Córdoba 'primitive'. The Puente Romano, the much-restored Roman bridge spanning the Río Guadalquivir, has at its south end the 14thC Torre de la Calahorra with splendid views downriver. Its multi-media installation recreates Moorish Córdoba (1030-1330, 1730-2000 Tue.-Sat., 1000-1400 Sun.; 250ptas). At the north end is the 16thC Puerta del Puente, built for King Philip II, (see **A-Z**) and the Baroque 18thC El Triumfo, with a statue of St. Raphael, patron saint of the city. The undoubted highlight of any visit is the Grand Mosque (Mezquita) itself, a superb architectural treasure (1000-1330, 1600-1900; 400ptas). Building began in AD 784 with successive expansions until 988. The forest of pillars with decorated capitals, about 850 in all from sites as far afield as the Middle East, and the innovative double tier of arches lead the visitor to the mihrab (prayer niche), exquisitely decorated with mosaics. After their Reconquest of the city in 1236, the Christians began transforming the Mosque into a church, culminating in the erection of an imposing Renaissance cathedral within the mosque's central area in the 16thC, a desecration condemned by Emperor Charles V (see **A-Z**). Southwest of the Mezquita is the 14thC Alcázar Nuevo (0930-1330, 1700-2000; 200ptas), built for King Alfonso XI and later a seat of the Inquisition. It now displays Roman and Moorish antiquities found on the site and its towers give views over the city. The attractive gardens are floodlit in summer (2200-2400). Northwest of the Alcázar is a well-preserved section of the city walls. The Moorish gateway, the Puerta de Almodóvar, leads into the attractive old Jewish quarter, the Judería, whose narrow streets extend to the Mezquita. c/ Judíos contains the Synagogue, built in the 14thC, which is *mudéjar* in style (1000-1400, 1530-1730 Tue.-Sat., 1000-1330 Sun.; 250ptas).

Return to Seville via Medina Azahara (1000-1400, 1800-2000 Tue.-Sat., 1000-1330 Sun.; 250ptas), site of the fabulous 10thC Moorish palace of Caliph Abderraman III, where excavations have enabled reconstruction of the Throne Room. Leave Córdoba by the C 431, turning right at the signpost for Medina Azahara (8 km).

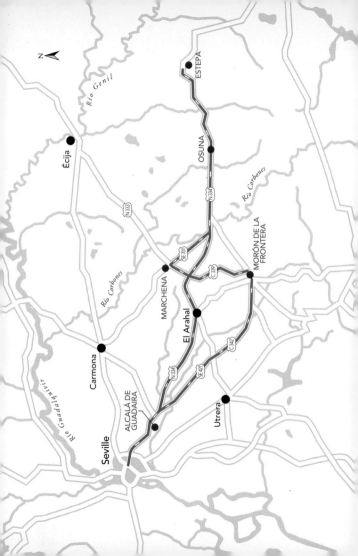

Hill Towns

*One very full day, or one and a half days with an overnight stay in
Osuna. The route includes minor roads and can be combined with*
EXCURSION 2 *by taking the C 430 from Osuna to Écija.*

Take the N 334 (signed Alcalá de Guadaira). Turn right onto the C 432.
15 km – Alcalá de Guadaira. Tourist information: Ayuntamiento (Town
Hall), Pl. del Duque 1. The 11-towered Moorish (see **A-Z**) castle (if
closed, ask at caretaker's house at entrance; free), was built in the
12thC to guard the approach to Seville. Although now in ruins it
remains a magnificent and imposing example of Almohade (see **A-Z**)
architecture. The massive dungeon was added in the 15thC. Continue
along the SE 421 and C 342.
62 km – Morón de la Frontera. A hill town topped by a ruined
Moorish castle. The steep streets reward the explorer with some fine
palacios and churches such as the Gothic (see **A-Z**) San Miguel with an
attractive minaret-inspired bell tower. However, Morón's most curious
monument, situated below the castle, is a plucked cock, El Gallo de
Morón, an irreverent memorial to a tax collector (the cock) sent to the
town who was stripped and humiliated by the indignant inhabitants!
Leave the town on the C 339 then follow the N 333 (signed Marchena).
88 km – Marchena. Tourist information: c/ San Francisco 2. The picturesque Moorish quarter built by the Almohades is still separated from
the rest of the town by a solid, well-preserved wall and entered by the
Puerta de la Rosa (Gate of the Rose). Among the churches are 15thC
Gothic San Juan Bautista, Gothic and *mudéjar* (see **A-Z**) Santa María de
la Mota which has unusual tiled decoration on the tower and, outside
the Moorish quarter, the grand 17thC Baroque (see **A-Z**) San Agustín,
which has Aztec and Inca detailing. From Marchena take the SE 701
then continue along the N 334.
122 km – Osuna. Tourist information: Ayuntamiento (Town Hall) Pl.
Mayor s/n. One of the architectural jewels of Andalucía, with a hilltop
setting dominated by the Old University and the collegiate church, La
Colegiata de Santa María de la Ascunción. Osuna was an important
Roman (see **A-Z**) town, and also has Visigothic (see **A-Z**) and Moorish
remains, but most of its rich architectural heritage, built by the Dukes of
Osuna, dates from the 16th-18thC. The University (0830-1500 Mon.-

Alcalá de Guadaira

Fri.; free), founded in 1549, has attractive tiled turrets and restrained Renaissance ornament. The building is now a school but its cloister with lecture and assembly halls, library, archives and oratory may be visited. Opposite is the Colegiata (1000-1300, 1600-1930 Tue.-Sat.; 150ptas), begun in 1534, with a beautiful Plateresque (see **A-Z**) patio and the private chapel and pantheon where the Dukes of Osuna are buried. Its sacristy museum has paintings commissioned by the Duke of Osuna from Ribera, while the church itself has a rich 18thC Baroque altarpiece. Downhill from the Colegiata is the Convent of La Encarnación begun in 1549 and now a museum (1000-1330, 1600-1930 Tue.-Sat.; 125ptas), whose patio (see **A-Z**) has an impressive dado of 18thC Seville tiles (see **Ceramics**). Around the centre of the town, near the *mercado* (market), are a number of interesting churches and public buildings, including the Audiencia (Court). There are also some exceptionally fine aristocratic houses, notably those in c/ San Pedro. Further uphill from the centre, towards the University, an archaeological museum (1000-1330, 1600-1930 Tue.-Sat.; 125ptas) with Iberian, Roman and Visigothic displays, is housed in the Torre del Agua or Torre Cartagines, the Carthaginian water tower. Continue on the N 334.

146 km – Estepa. Tourist information: Ayuntamiento (Town Hall), Pl. del Carmen 1. Another attractive hill town, originally an Iberian stronghold, captured by the Romans and later by the Moors. Its ruined hilltop Alcázar and tower have good views. Other buildings of interest include churches such as the Gothic Santa María la Mayor and the later Nuestra Señora del Carmen, as well as the Baroque Palacio de los Cerverales. Estepa is also famous for its *polvorones* (shortcake biscuits). Return to Seville on the N 334 (112 km).

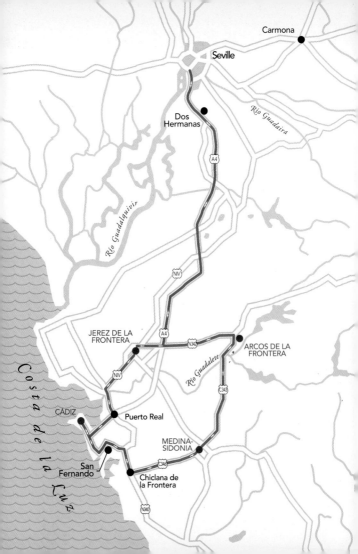

A two-day excursion including an overnight stay in Cádiz.

Take the N IV (signposted Jerez and Cádiz) to Dos Hermanas, where the *autopista* (motorway) A4 begins, exiting at Junction 4.

97 km – Jerez de la Frontera. Tourist information: Patronato Municipal de Turismo, Alameda Cristina 7. The word 'sherry' (see **A-Z**) is simply an anglicization of *jerez*. The famous wine has been exported to Britain for centuries and many of the traditional sherry producers, such as Sandeman, came originally from Britain. Other famous names include Domecq and González Byass. A tour of a sherry bodega and some tasting is the top priority for most visitors to Jerez. The bodegas are open for visits 1030-1330 Mon.-Fri. Jerez is also famous for horses and the city is particularly lively during the Horse Fair in May. The Real Escuela Andaluza de Arte Ecuestre gives displays of horsemanship every Thu. at 1200 (1500ptas) and its stables can be visited 1100-1300 weekdays. Jerez's important buildings include the restored 11thC Alcázar (1030-1330; free), with a Christianized mosque and attractive gardens, the 17thC Catedral (open for Mass 1800; free) and the beautiful Cabildo Municipal, the old Town Hall built in the 16thC in a mixture of *mudéjar* (see **A-Z**) and Plateresque (see **A-Z**) styles. Nearby are the Church of San Dionisio, 13thC with a Rococo altarpiece, and the Torre de la Atalaya. To the southeast is the 15thC Gothic (see **A-Z**) Church of San Miguel with a later tiled facade. The old quarter, with winding streets, orange trees and pretty patios (see **A-Z**), extends to the northwest, around the Church of San Lucas, and beyond are stretches of the Moorish (see **A-Z**) walls. Fine *palacios* include the Palacio Domecq. The clock museum, Museo de Relojes, has 300 timepieces (1000-1800 Mon.-Fri.; 200ptas). The bars round the centre and old quarter provide more opportunities for sampling sherry and *tapas* and there are many restaurants, including good fried-fish restaurants, *freidurías de pescado.* Continue on the N IV (signposted Cádiz), turning right at Puerto Real onto the CA 610 which bridges the entrance to the Bay of Cádiz.

138 km – Cádiz. Tourist information: c/ Calderón de la Barca 2. Situated on the promontory guarding the wide bay, Cádiz has been an important defensive site as well as a port for the Phoenicians, Carthaginians, Romans (see **A-Z**), Moors (see **A-Z**) and Christians. It

Jerez de la Frontera

flourished as a port in the 17thC, when it won from Seville the monopoly on Spanish trade with the Americas, while in the 18th-19thC British and Irish merchants settled there, many of them sherry exporters. Cádiz remains a busy port with a lively atmosphere. Medieval bastions protect the maze of the old town from the sea; promenades with wide sea views offer pleasant walks. The Museo de Cádiz (0930-1400 Tue.-Sun.; 250ptas) has important paintings, including the series of saints painted by Zurbarán (see **A-Z**) for the Carthusian monastery outside Jerez. Archaeological displays include Phoenician and Roman pieces. The 18thC chapel, La Capilla de la Santa Cueva (1000-1300 Mon.-Sat.; 50ptas), with an entrance on c/ Rosario, has frescoes by Goya, rare examples of the artist's religious work. The city has two cathedrals, the 'old' and the 'new'. The 18thC domed Catedral Nueva (1000-1300 Mon.-Sat.; 100ptas) dominates the wide Pl. de la Catedral and is a good example of local stonework, while the yellow tiles of the dome are also distinctive. The Cathedral treasures – paintings, silver and rich vest-ments – are in the Museum (1000-1300 Mon.-Sat.; 100ptas) entered at the side. The Catedral Vieja, originally dating from the 13thC but large-ly rebuilt in the 17thC, is beyond to the southeast. Cádiz has pleasant shopping streets and many bars and restaurants. Fish is extremely fresh and the various species caught around the salt marshes (Las Salinas) are a speciality. Again, take the N IV (signposted Jerez, Sevilla) out of Cádiz via San Fernando and the salt marshes, turning right after 22 km onto the N 340 (signposted Algeciras) then taking the C 346 at Chiclana.

186 km – Medina-Sidonia. The seat of the Dukes of Medina-Sidonia, the 7th of whom led the ill-fated Spanish Armada. As well as the Palacio Medina-Sidonia, there are attractive 15th-16thC buildings, including the Ayuntamiento (Town Hall). Some of the town's defensive walls and an arch remain. Follow the CA 204, which joins the C 343.

223 km – Arcos de la Frontera. Arcos is spectacularly situated on the winding Río Guadalete with picturesque steep streets and magnificent clifftop views. One of the best lookout points is just east of the main street, near the castle. Nearby are also the Parador, the Ayuntamiento and the Church of Santa María de la Asunción, which has 15thC wall paintings. Perched on the cliff is the Church of San Pedro. Take the N 342, following the signs for Sevilla at its junction with the A 4.

MUSEO ARQUEOLÓGICO Pl. de América.

❏ 1000-1400 Tue.-Sun. ❏ 250ptas.

Star attraction is the 8thC BC gold treasure from Carambolo. Also important Roman finds from Itálica and other sites near Seville. See A-Z.

MUSEO DE ARTES Y COSTUMBRES POPULARES
Pl. de América.

❏ 1000-1400 Tue.-Sat. ❏ 250ptas.

Interesting displays include costumes, musical instruments, ceramics, replica rooms and utensils. See WALK 4.

ARCHIVO GENERAL DE LAS INDIAS Av de la Constitución.

❏ 1000-1300 Mon.-Sat. ❏ Free.

Displays of original maps, letters, royal decrees, etc. in the Lonja (see BUILDINGS 1) relating to the discovery of America and Spain's colonization of it. See A-Z.

MUSEO DE BELLAS ARTES Pl. del Museo.

❏ 1000-1400, 1700-2000 Tue.-Fri., 1000-1400 Sat. & Sun. ❏ 250ptas.

Beautiful Renaissance monastery with an extremely important collection of works by Seville's Golden Age masters. See A-Z.

MUSEO DE ARTE CONTEMPORÁNEO c/ Santo Tomás.

❏ 1000-1400 Tue.-Sun. ❏ 250ptas.

20thC Spanish painting, sculpture and tapestry, from Miró, Tàpies and Saura to the new Andalucían talents.

MUSEO-CASA DE MURILLO c/ Santa Teresa.

❏ 1000-1400 Tue.-Sun. ❏ 250ptas.

Murillo's (see A-Z) house in the Barrio de Santa Cruz, furnished in traditional style and displaying paintings attributed to him and his followers.

MUSEO NÁUTICO Paseo de Cristóbal Colón.

❏ 1000-1400 Tue.-Sat., 1000-1300 Sun. ❏ 150ptas.

This small collection in the Torre del Oro (see BUILDINGS 1) gives an insight into Seville's role as an important river port.

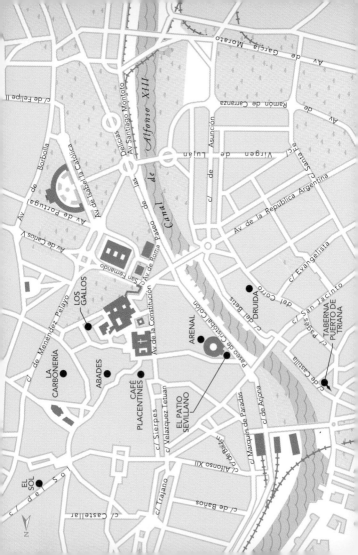

EL PATIO SEVILLANO Paseo de Cristóbal Colón 11, tel: 4214120.
❑ Shows at 1930, 2130, 2330.
Performers change but this tablao flamenco *is usually lively and profes-sional and sometimes includes folk songs and classical guitar pieces.*

LOS GALLOS Pl. de Santa Cruz 11, tel: 4216981.
❑ 2100-early morning.
*Attractive flamenco (see **A-Z**) venue in the Barrio de Santa Cruz, with a smartly-dressed clientele.*

ARENAL c/ Rodó 7, tel: 4216492.
❑ 2100-early morning.
The Tablao Flamenco de Curro Velez presents a good, professional show.

TABERNA PUERTO DE TRIANA c/ de Castilla 137.
❑ 2200-early morning.
One of the best places to enjoy or even try out the sevillanas *(see **A-Z**) dances, now so fashionable again among Seville's young people.*

LA CARBONERÍA c/ de Levies 18.
Attractive old building housing popular student bar which stays open till about 0400; sometimes has live music and art exhibitions. See **WALK 2**.

CAFÉ PLACENTINES c/ de Francos Placentines 2.
Old-world café; often has classical guitar performances after about 2300.

EL SOL c/ del Sol 40.
This bar's sessions from about 2300 draw the city's jazz enthusiasts.

ABADES c/ Abades 13.
*Beautiful old house with a charming patio (see **A-Z**), where elegant peo-ple gather for late-night drinks to the accompaniment of classical music.*

DRUIDA c/ Rodrigo de Triana 96.
Old-time café atmosphere in a modern setting, sometimes with live music. A good place to begin a night out.

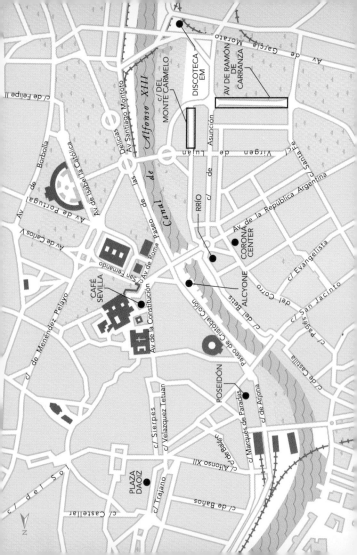

c/ DEL MONTE CARMELO

This plaza has numerous bars and open-air terrazas serving drinks, tapas *and meals until about 0200; especially popular with young people.*

PLAZA DAOIZ

A good choice of bars around this pretty square, from the traditional Bodega Doñana to modern bars like Gris; lively till the early hours.

CORONA CENTER c/ Pagés del Corro s/n.

❑ Till 0200.
Modern complex with eating, drinking and entertainment, from pizzas to a champagne bar and sometimes flamenco (see **A-Z**) *in La Raya Real.*

AV DE RAMÓN DE CARRANZA

Street of modern late-night music bars in Los Remedios district.

RRÍO c/ del Betis 67.

❑ 2000-0500 Tue.-Thu., 2000-2400 (teenagers), 2400-0700 (adults) Fri.-Sun. ❑ 500ptas.
A large discotheque which plays the latest mainstream music, with a balcony from which to watch the animated, young crowd.

DISCOTECA EM Av de García Morato s/n.

❑ 2000-0500 Thu.-Sun. ❑ 500ptas.
Large disco with a pleasant terraza *attracts a mixture of age groups.*

POSEIDÓN c/ Marqués de Paradas s/n.

Disco and bar in a lofty interior patio with imaginative lighting.

ALCYONE Paseo Alcalde Marqués de Contadero.

❑ Departs 2200.
Late-night cruise boat with discotheque, bars and a good mix of people.

CAFÉ SEVILLA c/ Miguel Mañara 9.

This late-night café with a pleasant atmosphere stays open till about 0300.

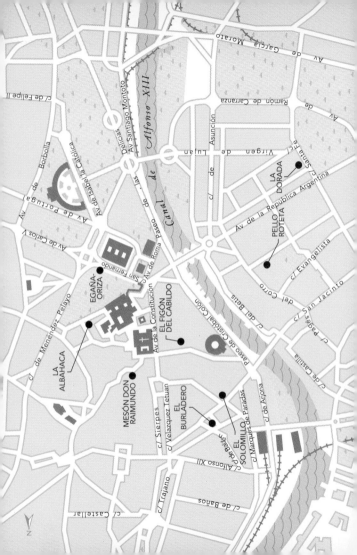

EGAÑA-ORIZA c/ San Fernando 41, tel: 4227211/54.
❑ See **Opening Times**. Closed Sat. lunch, Sun. & Aug. ❑ Expensive.
One of the city's top restaurants, serving Basque and international cuisine of the highest standard, with smart service and elegant decor.

LA DORADA c/ Virgen de Aguas Santas 6, tel: 4455110.
❑ See **Opening Times**. Closed Sun. ❑ Expensive.
Seville's best fish and seafood restaurant, recommended by Sevillians. Saltbaked fish, pescado a la sal, is exceptional. Excellent service.

LA ALBAHACA Pl. de Santa Cruz 12, tel: 4220714.
❑ See **Opening Times**. Closed Sun. ❑ Moderate-Expensive.
A beautiful old house in the Barrio de Santa Cruz. The food is Andalusian, imaginative and delicate and the service is attentive.

EL BURLADERO Hotel Tryp Colón, c/ Canalejas 1, tel: 4222900.
❑ See **Opening Times**. Closed Sun. ❑ Moderate-Expensive.
Good local and international cuisine, in andaluz-style surroundings.

EL FIGÓN DEL CABILDO Pl. del Cabildo s/n, tel: 4220117.
❑ See **Opening Times**. Closed Sun. eve. ❑ Moderate-Expensive.
Creative modern cooking with good fish and seafood dishes.

MESÓN DON RAIMUNDO c/ Argote de Molina 26, tel: 4223355.
❑ See **Opening Times**. Closed Sun. eve. ❑ Moderate.
Traditional andaluz dishes and new-style cooking served in a converted convent.

PELLO ROTETA c/ Farmacéutico E. M. Herrera 10, tel: 4278417.
❑ See **Opening Times**. Closed Sun. & mid Aug.-mid Sep. ❑ Moderate.
Quiet and tasteful family-run restaurant offering traditional and modern Basque cuisine.

EL SOLOMILLO c/ Santas Patronas 3, tel: 4222209.
❑ See **Opening Times**. Closed Sun. eve. ❑ Moderate.
A cosy restaurant serving good Basque home-cooking.

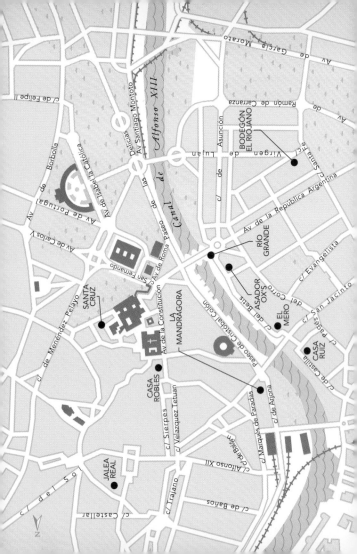

CASA ROBLES c/ Alvarez Quintero 58, tel: 4223150.
❑ See **Opening Times**. ❑ Moderate.
Delicious andaluz cooking makes it a favourite with Sevillians.

RÍO GRANDE c/ del Betis 70, tel: 4278371/4273936.
❑ See **Opening Times**. ❑ Moderate.
Popular international menu and a wonderful view across the river.

ASADOR OX'S c/ del Betis 61, tel: 4279585.
❑ See **Opening Times**. Closed Sun. eve. & Aug. ❑ Moderate.
Quality meats prepared in simple Basque and Navarrese style.

BODEGÓN EL RIOJANO c/ Virgen de las Montañas 12,
tel: 4450682.
❑ See **Opening Times**. ❑ Moderate.
A traditional mesón-style restaurant specializing in meat dishes.

EL MERO c/ del Betis 1-3, tel: 4338549.
❑ See **Opening Times**. Closed Tue. ❑ Moderate.
One of the many restaurants in Triana specializing in fish.

SANTA CRUZ Pl. de los Venerables s/n.
❑ See **Opening Times**. ❑ Inexpensive-Moderate.
Popular restaurant with terraza serving traditional favourites.

CASA RUIZ c/ de Castilla 3, tel: 4333091.
❑ See **Opening Times**. Closed Tue. ❑ Inexpensive-Moderate.
Lively ambience with specials including rabo de toro (bull's tail).

LA MANDRÁGORA c/ Albuera 11, tel: 4220184.
❑ See **Opening Times**. Closed Sun.-Wed. eve. ❑ Inexpensive-Moderate.
Imaginative vegetarian cooking and delicious desserts.

JALEA REAL c/ Sor Ángela de la Cruz 37.
❑ See **Opening Times**. Closed Sat. eve & Sun. ❑ Inexpensive.
Good, functional vegetarian café-restaurant.

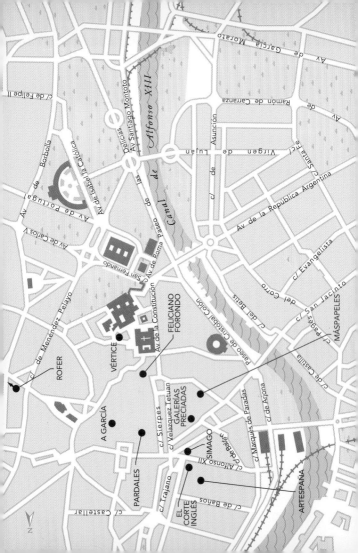

EL CORTE INGLÉS Pl. del Duque s/n.
A branch of Spain's top chain of department stores, it has a full range of departments and services, including a good supermarket.

GALERÍAS PRECIADAS Pl. Magdalena Campaña s/n.
A cheaper version of El Corte Inglés, its main store is on one side of the square and household goods on the other.

SIMAGO Pl. del Duque s/n.
Across from El Corte Inglés, a much lower-priced department store and supermarket.

FELICIANO FORONDO c/ Alvarez Quintero 52.
Probably the best place to buy beautiful Spanish shawls and mantillas.

PARDALES c/ de la Cuna 23.
*Specializes in the tiered sevillanas (see **A-Z**) dresses worn at the Feria de Abril (see **A-Z**).*

ROFER Av de la Prensa 31.
*A shop specializing in the traditional male costumes worn at the Feria de Abril (see **A-Z**) and the pilgrimage to El Rocío (see **Rocío**).*

A GARCÍA c/ Alcaicería 29.
Men's hat shop selling the traditional wide-brimmed Andalusian sombreros worn at the ferias.

VÉRTICE c/ Mateos Gago 24a.
General bookshop which always has a good stock of books in English.

ARTESPAÑA Pl. Gavidia 1.
A branch of a national chain selling high-quality crafts and design items.

MÁSPAPELES c/ Zaragoza 17.
Modern designs made of paper and other imaginative gifts. Always a useful stop for last-minute presents.

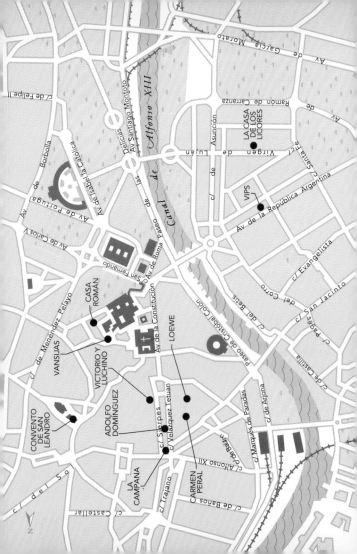

LA CASA DE LOS LICORES c/ Virgen de Luján 35.
Excellent selection of fine Spanish wines, liqueurs and spirits, plus many imports.

CASA ROMÁN Pl. de los Venerables.
A wonderful Sevillian oddity – a delicatessen where you can buy local specialities to take away or to consume in the adjoining bar. See **WALK 1**.

LA CAMPANA c/ Sierpes 1.
One of many places which sell mouthwatering pastries, cakes and other delicious confections.

CONVENTO DE SAN LEANDRO Pl. de San Leandro.
The nuns support themselves by making and selling their yemas, *sweets made from egg yolk according to a secret recipe. See* **WALK 2**.

VIPS Av de la República Argentina 23.
One of a successful chain of American-style drugstores with a film-processing service, cafeteria and restaurant, all open until 0300.

LOEWE Pl. Nueva 13.
Elegant leather clothing and accessories are specialities of this famous Spanish fashion house. Expensive but top quality.

ADOLFO DOMÍNGUEZ c/ Rioja 1.
Designs by one of the stars of modern Spanish fashion.

CARMEN PERAL c/ Muñoz Olive 5.
An exclusive boutique for women's clothing and footwear by leading Spanish designers.

VICTORIO Y LUCHINO c/ Sierpes 87.
Exuberant young Spanish designer-clothes and accessories.

VANSIJAS Pasaje Andreu 3.
Amazing earrings, painted masks and other modern design items.

EL RINCONCILLO c/ Gerona 1, Campana.
Seville's oldest bar, over 300 years old and packed with character, serves fine hams and a choice of wines.

EL PATIO c/ San Eloy 9, Campana.
Lots of hanging hams and a special black beer. On the same street is El Rincón, with a typical Sevillian patio (see **A-Z**) *and plenty of tapas.*

BAR EL VALLE Av de Alvar Nuñez 18.
This bar has a warm, family feel. Pez espada (swordfish) is the speciality.

BAR LA GIRALDA c/ Mateos Gago 1, Centro.
Attractive tiled interior and a good range of tapas and raciones (larger portions).

CASA PACO c/ Madre Rafols 6, Los Remedios.
Bullfighting posters decorate this bar which serves its tapas on paper.

BAR LOS MELLIZOS c/ Virgen de las Montañas s/n, Los Remedios.
Family-run bar with a wide choice of tapas. Try las bombas, meat-filled potatoes.

BODEGA MANTUA c/ Pagés del Corro 45, Triana.
Typical of the old-style bars in Triana. Tapas served here include caracoles (snails).

RUPERTO Av de Santa Cecilia 2, Triana.
Lots of atmosphere here; the codornices (quails) from northern Spain are the most popular speciality – over 2000 of them are served every week.

BODEGA SIGLO XVIII c/ Pelay Correa 32, Triana.
A fascinating old building. The tasty patatas ali-oli (garlic potatoes) are recommended.

LA PRIMERA DEL PUENTE c/ del Betis 66, Triana.
Order pieces of battered cod (pavías) at the bar or on the terrace.

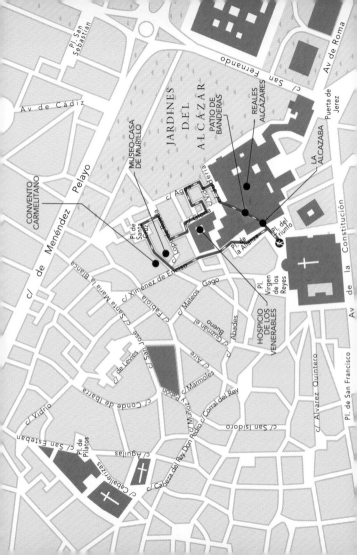

Pl. San Sebastián

Av de Cádiz

de Menéndez Pelayo

CONVENTO CARMELITANO

C/ de

C/ Fabiola

C/ Santa María la Blanca

C/ Ximénez de Enciso

C/ San José

C/ Vidrio

Pl. de San Esteban

C/ San Esteban

C/ Caballerizas

C/ Conde de Ibarra

C/ de Levíes

C/ Aguilas

C/ Cabeza del Rey Don Pedro

C/ Muñoz y Pabón

C/ Mármoles

C/ Arte

C/ Guzmán el Bueno

C/ Abades

C/ Mateos Gago

Pl. de Santa Cruz

C/ López Rueda

MUSEO-CASA DE MURILLO

JARDINES DEL ALCÁZAR

PATIO DE BANDERAS

REALES ALCAZARES

Av de Roma

C/ de San Fernando

Puerta de Jerez

LA ALCAZABA

Pl. del Triunfo

Pl. de la Alianza

Pl. Virgen de los Reyes

HOSPICIO DE LOS VENERABLES

Av de la Constitución

C/ Corral del Rey

C/ San Isidoro

C/ Álvarez Quintero

Pl. de San Francisco

Barrio de Santa Cruz

1-1.5 hr, including visits.

Begin at Pl. del Triunfo (near the Cathedral). Pass under the arch, La Alcazaba, at the eastern side of the Alcázar walls to enter the Patio de Banderas (see **Patios**), pleasantly shaded by orange trees. Its enclosed atmosphere signals the start of the Barrio de Santa Cruz, originally part of the self-contained, walled quarter for Seville's sizable Jewish population (see **Jews**). Exit by the roofed street, c/ Judería, at the far left end. Turn left into its continuation and exit by an arched gateway, one of several by which Jews had access to the rest of the city. Turn right into c/ Vida (Street of Life), where some of the houses have pretty miradores (lookout galleries). Turn left into c/ Agua (Water Street), which once had a little aqueduct running along the right-hand wall, and left into c/ Pimienta (Pepper Street), typical of the barrio's narrow streets of white-washed houses with balconies colourful with pots of flowers. Thick walls keep out the summer heat and the cooler interior patios, occasionally glimpsed through ironwork rejas (see **A-Z**), become the focus of the houses. The great Spanish actress, María Guerrero, once lived at No. 14. Opposite is the site of the original Hostería del Laurel, immortalized by Zorrilla in his 19thC version of the Don Juan (see **A-Z**) story, Don Juan Tenorio. Go left into c/ Susona, named after a Jewish girl who betrayed her father, leader of a proposed 15thC rebellion, to her Christian lover. Deserted by him, she died in shame, having asked, so the story goes, that her skull be put above the door of her house. At No. 10a a ceramic tile with a skull is a reference to the legend. c/ Susona leads into the pretty Pl. de Doña Elvira, which was once used as a theatre for comedies. The Bordados Artesanía (textile workshop – see **CRAFTS**), one of the barrio's numerous artesanías, is in this square. Enter Pl. de los Venerables by way of c/ Gloria to visit the 17thC Hospicio de los Venerables (see **BUILDINGS 2**), built for retired priests and whose church has paintings by Seville painters Valdés Leal (see **A-Z**) and Lucas Valdés. Also in this square are Casa Román (see **SHOPPING 2**) and the new Hostería del Laurel, both good stopping points for a drink and tapas. Leaving the square by c/ Reinoso, turn right into c/ Lope de Rueda (both named after poets), passing on the left at No. 21 a 16thC doorway with fine Renaissance and Gothic (see **A-Z**) motifs. Enter Pl. Alfaro where Figaro, in Rossini's The Barber of Seville, serenaded the

beautiful Rosina on her balcony. A grand *palacio* is at No. 4. Adjoining Pl. Alfaro is the Pl. de Santa Cruz, previously the site of the church where the painter Murillo (see **A-Z**) was buried and which gave its name to the *barrio*. The church was destroyed by Napoleon's troops during the Peninsular War (see **A-Z**). The square contains a fine 17thC wrought-iron cross. Exit left into c/ Santa Teresa, named after the 16thC Spanish mystic saint and poet who founded the Carmelite convent in this street. Its church is open before and after services. The Museo-Casa de Murillo (see **MUSEUMS**), Murillo's house, is also in this street. The house and central patio are typical of the *barrio*, while the paintings, mainly by followers, give an idea of the important influence of the artist on the Seville School. Turn left into c/ Ximénez de Enciso. On the right is c/ Mesón del Moro, so named because in 1491 a Moor was given leave to open eating places here. Follow c/ Ximénez de Enciso and Pasaje Andreu, turning left into c/ Rodrigo Caro to reach the Pl. de la Alianza, a pleasant spot by the Alcázar walls. Leave by c/ Romero Morube to finish at Pl. del Triunfo.

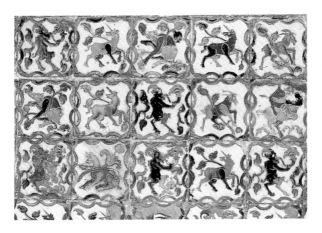

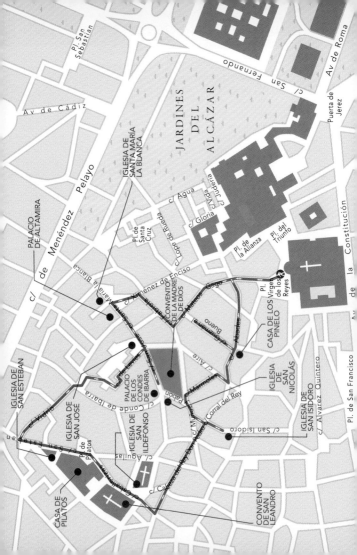

Barrio de San Bartolomé

1-1.5 hr, excluding visits.

Start from Pl. Virgen de los Reyes. Cross the plaza to enter c/ Mateos Gago, with superb vistas of the Giralda (see **BUILDINGS 1**). A short way up the hill, turn left up steps at the entrance to c/ Abades which winds tortuously at the beginning. Although much of this area was redeveloped in the 16thC, the streets still follow the maze-like plan of the earlier Jewish quarter (see **Jews**). Traffic is still permitted in most of this area, so be alert. Millstones incorporated at the base of several houses to protect against damage from horses and carriages show that through traffic was a problem even in earlier times! Popular tradition has it that many of the houses in c/ Abades (Street of the Abbots) were built for mistresses of the clergy, while another story claims that here the 14thC King Pedro the Cruel murdered a rival for the affections of one of his mistresses. Most houses, however, were built for rich merchants in the 16th and 17thC. Several have a mirador (lookout tower) or an arched gallery at the top based on Italian Renaissance models, and there are some pretty patios (see **A-Z**), e.g. at No. 33. Turn right into c/ Guzmán el Bueno, named after a Christian hero of the Reconquest who gained the name 'the Good' for sacrificing his son to the infidel! Marble portals on some of the houses also show 16thC Italian influence. The best example is at No. 4, with the dates 1560, 1654 and 1856 recording building and restorations. The rest of the house is typically Sevillian, with a spacious, semi-covered entrance area for horses and vehicles and, beyond, a covered entrance hall with wrought-iron grille (see **Rejas**) affording a glimpse of a beautiful tiled patio. Return to c/ Abades, where the grandest house, with a delightful arcaded mirador, is No. 12-14, the 16thC Casa de los Pinelo which now houses Seville's Academies of Letters and Fine Arts. The Pinelo family, one of many of Genoese origin in Seville, were bankers to Emperor Charles V (see **A-Z**). Still on c/ Abades, turn right into c/ Aire and take the left fork, c/ Mármoles, where three massive Roman columns, possibly from Itálica (see **EXCURSION 1**), present a most unexpected sight. Exit left into c/ Muñoz y Pabón, first left into c/ Perla, left into c/ Corral del Rey, and first right into c/ San Isidoro to reach the 14thC Church of San Isidoro (open before and after services), dedicated to the Visigothic (see **A-Z**) Bishop Isidore, one of the city's patron saints. Its altarpiece is by 17thC

Seville painter Juan de las Roelas. Return to c/ Corral del Rey and continue left along it and take the right fork at c/ Cabeza del Rey Don Pedro. Cross c/ Águilas and continue along c/ Cabeza del Rey Don Pedro, turning right and immediately left into c/ Alhóndiga to reach the Pl. de San Leandro and the Renaissance Convent of the same name, designed by Juan de Oviedo at the beginning of the 17thC. The nuns here sell home-made sweets (see **SHOPPING 2**). c/ San Ildefonso leads off from the plaza into Pl. San Ildefonso, where towers the recently restored church of the same name (open before and after services), with a facade of monumental proportions dating from its 18thC rebuilding, and containing a 14thC fresco. Turn left down c/ Caballerizas which leads into Pl. de Pilatos with, on the right, a statue commemorating the painter Zurbarán (see **A-Z**) and, on the left, the entrance to Casa de Pilatos (see **BUILDINGS 1**). The splendid triumphal gateway erected in 1533 was commissioned by the 1st Marquis of Tarifa from the Genoese sculptor Antonio Aprile and shipped to Seville, where it started the fashion for Italian stonework. The strange Crusaders' crosses above and their inscriptions record the Marquis' visit to Jerusalem in 1519. Just beyond Pl. de Pilatos in c/ San Esteban is the little 14th-15thC Church of San Esteban (open before and after services) in Gothic (see **A-Z**) and *mudéjar* (see **A-Z**) style, containing paintings of St. Peter and St. Paul by Zurbarán. One of the gates of the city, the Puerta de Carmona, formerly stood at the end of this street. It also divided Judería (Jewish quarter) on the right from Morería (Moorish quarter) on the left, when Moors (see **A-Z**) under Christian rule (*moriscos*) were, like the Jews, restricted to a specific area of the city. Turn right at c/ Vidrío to re-enter part of the Jewish quarter, the Barrio de San Bartolomé, less salubrious but more authentic than the Barrio de Santa Cruz. At the end, turn into Pl. de los Mercedarias, dominated by the late *mudéjar*-style Colegio de los Mercedarias. Cross the square and turn right into the winding c/ de Levies, named after one of Seville's most influential Jews, Samuel Levi, treasurer to King Pedro the Cruel. The street has lost some of its elegant houses, such as the 17thC house of Miguel de Mañara, founder of the Hospital de la Caridad (see **Caridad**), although at No. 18 is a more modest but pleasing building, La Carbonería (coal merchant's), transformed into a popular bar (see **NIGHTLIFE 1**). Exit into Pl. San José, containing the church of the same name, and turn right into c/ San José where, a little way up on the right at No. 3, is the grand 17th-18thC house of the Counts of Ibarra, now belonging to the Junta de Andalucía (Andalusian government), where an open door usually permits a view of the rich *azulejos* (tiles) and fine woodwork. Across the street is the Convento de la Madre de Díos, occupied by an enclosed order of nuns and built in the 16thC on ground confiscated for the Crown when the Jews were expelled. Ahead is the Church of San Nicolás. Turning back down c/ San José to its continuation as c/ Santa María la Blanca, the imposing Baroque (see **A-Z**) facade of the huge and recently renovated Palacio de Altamira is at No. 1 on the left and now houses the Consejería de Cultura, the Cultural Department of the Junta de Andalucía. Further down on the left is the Church of Santa María la Blanca (open for Mass 1030 & 1930 Mon.-Sat., 1000, 1130, 1230 & 1900 Sun.), once a synagogue but with few hints of this now remaining in its stunning Baroque interior. It contains paintings by 17thC Sevillian artists including Murillo (see **A-Z**). This street was formerly one of the principal thoroughfares of the Jewish quarter. At the end of it stood another of Seville's gates by which Jews were permitted to enter and leave the city. Return to c/ Mateos Gago by turning back up c/ Santa María la Blanca, crossing over where it widens opposite the Palacio de Altamira and turning right up c/ Fabiola and left into c/ Mateos Gago.

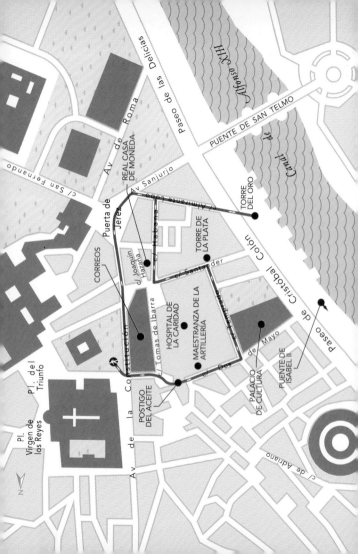

Arenal

1.5 hr, including visits.

Start outside the Lonja (see **BUILDINGS 1**) in Av de la Constitución. Cross the avenue, turning down c/ Almirantazgo at the right-hand end of the Correos building (main post office). This street leads into Arenal, the old port area of Seville, once bustling with the activities of building and refitting ships and of loading and unloading the Indies fleets, their cargoes including the fabulous quantities of gold and silver which entered Spain in the 16th and 17thC. The Renaissance archway at the end of the street is the Postigo del Aceite, the oil gate. Its inscription records its construction in the 16thC, paid for by various olive oil producers including the Counts of Ibarra, still producers today. Olive oil has been an important crop in Andalucía since earliest times and was one of the major exports to the Spanish colonies. The Postigo del Aceite is the only remaining gate of several that protected the port area, each assigned to a different product. The gates also provided protection for the rest of the city, particularly the Cathedral, against the many floods of the Río Guadalquivir (see **A-Z**). On the right just before the arch is a little altarpiece. Through the gate in c/ Dos de Mayo, the building on the left with eight arched windows is the 18thC Maestranza de la Artillería, formerly the Royal Arsenal during the Age of Discovery (see **A-Z**). Turn left into c/ Temprado, passing the entrance of the Maestranza. The whole of the left-hand side of the street was originally occupied by the Moorish (see **A-Z**) shipyards (*Atarazanas*), whose layout is still suggested by the strange-shaped windows of the Maestranza. On the right, extending towards the river, is the new theatre complex, the Palacio de Cultura. Further along on the left is the Hospital de la Caridad (see **BUILDINGS 1**) whose fascinating Church of San Jorge was completed in 1670. One of the interior patios (see **A-Z**) of the Hospital still retains remains of the arches of the *Atarazanas*. A statue of Miguel de Mañara, founder of the Hospital, who also commissioned the Church's paintings by Murillo (see **A-Z**) and Valdés Leal (see **A-Z**), is in the gardens opposite. Exit into c/ Santander where the top of the Torre de la Plata (Silver Tower), less well-known than the Torre del Oro, is just visible above the surrounding buildings. Although much altered, it was possibly built for defensive purposes in the 13thC. Turn left up c/ Santander where, on the right, on the corner with c/ Joaquín Hazaña, is

the partially restored Real Casa de Moneda (Royal Mint), built in 1575, although the present facade is 18thC. During the heyday of Seville's monopoly of trade with the colonies in the Indies, huge quantities of gold and silver were stored here, much of it melted down for coins. Pass beneath the archway (c/ Habana) to the arcaded interior courtyard which once had gateways on each side so that the whole building could be closed off. Exit ahead into c/ Almirante Lobo and turn right. At the end, on the riverside, is the Torre del Oro (see **BUILDINGS 1**), built by the Almohades (see **A-Z**), the last Moorish rulers of Seville, at the beginning of the 13thC to defend the river approach to the city. It was once linked by walls to the Torre de la Plata and the Reales Alcázares. Its name, the Gold Tower, is thought to refer to the gold-coloured reflections created by the *azulejos* (tiles) which once covered the exterior, or to the fact that it guarded stores of gold in the time of King Pedro the Cruel. The stretch of river between the two bridges, the Puente de San Telmo on the left and the Puente de Isabel II on the right, formed the area of the docks in previous centuries, with the Puente de Isabel II replacing a bridge of boats only in the 19thC. The present Seville docks are further downriver. Now canalized as the Canal Alfonso XIII and with no boats other than the excursion boats and pleasure craft, it gives little impression of past activity. Return to Av de la Constitución via c/ Almirante Lobo.

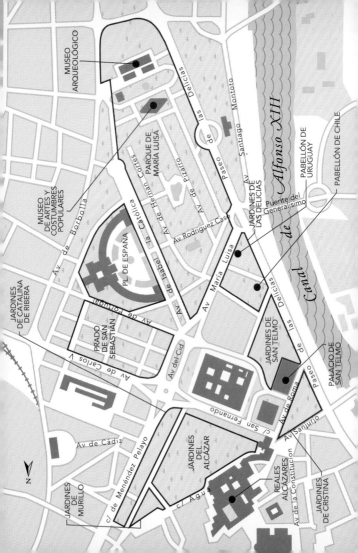

Gardens & Parks

3 hr, excluding visits.

Southeast of the Reales Alcázares (see **BUILDINGS 1**) is a huge area of attractively laid-out public gardens and parks ideal for strolling and relaxing and screened from major traffic routes that divide up the area. Start in the Alcázar gardens (Jardines del Alcázar, entered only through the Reales Alcázares). Pleasant gardens are yet another legacy of Seville's Moorish past. In a hot climate, essential elements were running water, shade and fragrant plants. The formal gardens of the Alcázar, though much altered since Moorish times, still incorporate these in their layout, while the *mudéjar* (see **A-Z**) pavilion of Emperor Charles V (see **A-Z**), with a fountain, dome and decorated tilework, continues the Moorish style of garden architecture. The less formal gardens beyond contain a number of plants including prickly pears brought to Seville from the Indies, when, in the time of King Philip II (see **A-Z**), many of these newly-discovered plants were studied for their uses in medicine. Continue outside the walled Jardines del Alcázar into the Patio de Banderas (see **Patios**), taking c/ Judería, turning right into c/ Vida and left to the end of c/ Agua to reach the Jardines de Murillo. Bordering the Barrio de Santa Cruz, these are a modern continuation of traditional Moorish garden design, laid out earlier this century. Next to them, the Jardines de Catalina de Ribera, with a statue of Columbus (see **A-Z**), provide an effective screen from the busy c/ de Menéndez Pelayo. Across Pl. de Don Juan de Austria is the extensive Prado (meadow) de San Sebastián, containing an open-air auditorium where pop and classical concerts are frequently held in the summer. Beyond, in Av de Isabel la Católica, turn left into the wide and impressive Pl. de España (see **BUILDINGS 2**), built for the 1929 Ibero-American exhibition. Cross the avenue to the extensive and delightful Parque de María Luisa, also part of the exhibition site. At the southeast end on Pl. de América are the Museo Arqueológico (see **MUSEUMS**) and the Museo de Artes y Costumbres Populares (see **MUSEUMS**). Across Av María Luisa, in the smaller Jardines de las Delicias, the pavilions of Chile and Uruguay are used for concerts. The Jardines de las Delicias, like the Parque de María Luisa, were originally part of the grounds of the Palacio de San Telmo (see **San Telmo**), formerly owned by the Dukes of Montpensier. The Jardines de San Telmo behind the *palacio* are now also a public park.

Reales Alcázares

Accidents & Breakdowns: If you have an accident or break-down, you can summon assistance by 'phoning the operator, tel: 009, no coins required. It is best to join the AA or RAC or a similar motoring organization before you go on holiday for information on driving rules and conditions and advice on accident procedures. See **Consulates, Driving, Emergency Numbers, Police.**

Accommodation: The luxurious Hotel Alfonso XIII was built for the 1929 Ibero-American Exhibition and remains the city's top hotel. Other hotels include the big international-style ones, as well as smaller ones in beautiful old houses, while further down the range there are numer-ous family-run *hostales* and *pensiones*. Prices vary according to star rat-ing (one to five stars with Gran Lujo as extra-luxury) and season, and each room should display the applicable maximum charge inclusive of service and taxes. Guesthouses (*casas de huéspedes*) and inns (*fondas*) offer the most basic accommodation. Local tourist offices have lists of accommodation and prices and can offer assistance with finding

accommodation. Spain's national tourist offices abroad can also provide information (see **Tourist Information**). Accommodation in Seville during Semana Santa (see **A-Z**) and the Feria de Abril (see **A-Z**) must be booked months in advance. See **Camping & Caravanning**, **Paradores Nacionales**, **Youth Hostels**.

Admission Charges: These are correct when going to press but are generally increased each season. Most publicly funded buildings, such as museums, are free to EC nationals, subject to proof, e.g. passport.

Age of Discovery: Rodrigo de Triana of Seville, one of Columbus' (see **A-Z**) crew, was the first Spaniard to sight land in the New World in Oct. 1492. In 1519 Magellan and Elcano set sail from Seville on the voyage of global circumnavigation, and Cortés conquered Mexico's Aztecs. Pizarro took Peru and the riches of the Incas into Spanish possession in 1532. Annexation of major new territories of the Americas continued throughout the 16thC, bringing huge wealth to Spain. Seville, Spain's gateway to its rich, new empire, flourished and quickly doubled in size. See **Expo '92**.

Airport: San Pablo airport, 12 km east of the city on the main road N IV (E 25), has a capacity of 4300 passengers an hour. There are frequent direct flights to other Spanish cities and to many international destinations. The Spanish airline, Iberia, is the main operator and handling agent for other airlines. Its city office is at c/ Almirante Lobo 3, tel: 4228901, or for reservations, tel: 4218800. The airport bus terminus in the city is at Bar Iberia in c/ Almirante Lobo. Metered taxis (see **A-Z**) charge a supplement for journeys to and from the airport. For all airport information, tel: 4510677/4516111.

Alcázares, Reales: The Moors (see **A-Z**) captured Seville in 712 and built a fortress on this site. Further enlargements took place up to the 11thC. After the Christian Reconquest, the 14thC King Pedro the Cruel ordered the reconstruction of the royal palace, incorporating remains from the earlier Moorish (see **A-Z**) buildings, as well as employing *mudéjar* (see **A-Z**) craftsmen to continue traditional styles

and techniques in stuccowork and tiling (*azulejos*).
Later additions and alterations were carried out by the
Catholic Monarchs (see **A-Z**) Ferdinand and Isabel and
by Emperor Charles V (see **A-Z**) and his son Philip II
(see **A-Z**). These included the Sala de los Almirantes
(see **Casa de la Contratación**), the Chapel of Isabel
with tiles by Nicolás Pisano, and the apartments of
Charles V.
The *mudéjar* palace of Pedro the Cruel remains the
highlight of the visit. The Salón de Embajadores
(Ambassadors' Hall) with its magnificent gilded dome
has the greatest splendour, while the Patios de las
Doncellas and de las Muñecas (Courtyards of the
Maidens and of the Dolls) with their intricately pat-
terned stuccowork provide delightful vistas through
arches and doorways. The gardens, Jardines del Alcázar
(see **WALK 4**), have pleasant pools, pavilions and trees –
ideal for shade and relaxing. The Reales Alcázares continue to be the royal residence in Seville and may
occasionally close at short notice for royal visits. See
BUILDINGS 1.

Almohades: A strict, reforming Islamic sect from the
south of Morocco who conquered Andalucía in 1161
and established Seville as their capital in 1171-2. They built the beautiful Giralda (see **BUILDINGS 1**) and the defensive Torre del Oro (see
BUILDINGS 1), as well as the Alcázar at Alcalá de Guadaira (see **EXCUR-
SION 3**). With their decisive defeat by the Christians at the Battle of Las
Navas de Tolosa in 1212, their influence in Spain waned and in 1248
they lost Seville to King Ferdinand III (see **A-Z**).

Andalucía: The name comes from the Arabic *al-Andalus*, which was
in turn derived from the name given to the region by the Vandals in the
5thC. It is one of Spain's 17 autonomous regions with its own parliament and government, the Junta de Andalucía. Seville is its capital. Its
eight provinces stretch across the whole of southern Spain from Huelva

Reales Alcázares

and Cádiz on the Atlantic coast to Málaga, Granada and Almería provinces along the Mediterranean. Seville, Córdoba and Jaén are the inland provinces. In recent decades tourism has been a principal economic activity. The European Community's largest-ever regional development plan is targeted at Andalucía, while Seville's Expo '92 (see **A-Z**) has also generated foreign investment. Communications have improved in recent years, with new motorway, rail and air links and better telecommunications, power and water supplies. Manufacturing, construction and technical services have been growing fast, while agricultural crops and techniques have changed rapidly, with traditional grains and olives giving way to early fruit and vegetables, often grown under plastic sheeting. See **Orientation**.

Archivo General de las Indias: Juan de Herrera, favoured architect of Philip II (see **A–Z**), designed the building which displays an austere grandeur typical of his style. It was completed in 1598 to serve as
the Lonja (see **BUILDINGS 1**), after the Archbishop of Seville had com-
plained to the king about trading on the Cathedral steps, in the Patio de
Naranjos and even inside the Cathedral itself in bad weather! Since
1785, when King Charles III (see **A–Z**) established the archives, the
large rooms have built up a collection of over four million documents
relating to Spain's discovery of the New World and its administration of
its colonies via detailed plans and instructions sent out with the twice-
yearly fleets. Visitors may stroll among the imposing rows of documents
and glimpse their fascinating contents through the selection on display.
See **MUSEUMS, Casa de la Contratación**.

Arqueológico, Museo: Occupying two floors of the Renaissance-
style palace built for the 1929 Ibero-American Exhibition, its displays
cover Palaeolithic to Moorish (see **Moors**) times. The most stunning
and exciting exhibits are undoubtedly the 8thC BC Carambolo Treasure
discovered in 1958, delicate pieces of gold jewellery from the ancient
state of Tartessos (see **A–Z**), near Seville. There are also numerous
exhibits from the Roman site at Itálica (see **EXCURSION 1**), just outside
Seville. See **MUSEUMS, WALK 4**.

Ayuntamiento: The building of the Town Hall began in 1527 under
Diego de Riaño, one of the outstanding architects of the Plateresque
(see **A–Z**), the style most exuberantly displayed on the facade facing the
Pl. de San Francisco. It incorporates both Gothic (see **A–Z**) and
Renaissance motifs and figures, including those of Hercules (see **A–Z**),
mythical founder of the city, Julius Caesar, who made it an assize town,
and Emperor Charles V (see **A–Z**), during whose reign the building was
constructed. See **BUILDINGS 1**.

Baby-sitters: Make enquiries in advance through your travel agent
or tour operator. It is not the general practice for hotels to provide this
service and Seville has no official agency of professional baby-sitters.
See **Children**.

Banks: See **Currency, Money, Opening Times.**

Baroque: The dominant style in art and architecture in Spain during the 17thC and into the 18thC. Following on from the Renaissance styles, in architecture it is characterized by a love of complex curved and massive forms, as in the Iglesia de la Magdalena (see **BUILDINGS 2**). In the later High Baroque phase there is often an exuberant profusion of sculptural detailing, usually concentrated round doorways, as at the Palacio de San Telmo (see **San Telmo**). In painting Baroque is characterized by a new naturalism in composition and colouring, though there are often strong contrasts of light and shade. The supreme masters Zurbarán (see **A-Z**), Velázquez (see **A-Z**) and Murillo (see **A-Z**) all worked in Seville, while the dramatic compositions of Valdés Leal (see **A-Z**) and Francisco de Herrera the Younger exemplify the High Baroque there in the later 17thC.

Beaches: See **Costa de la Luz.**

Bellas Artes, Museo de: The Fine Arts Museum is housed in the magnificent Renaissance and Baroque (see **A-Z**) Convento de la Merced (Convent of Mercy) begun by the architect Juan de Oviedo in the 17thC. Its collection is extremely impressive, second only to that of the Prado, much of it rescued from other convents and monasteries in Seville after their dissolution in 1835. Examples of ceramic tiling (*azulejos*) and stonework are displayed and, in sculpture (see **A-Z**), some of the polychromed wood figures so peculiar to Spain. In paintings, the Spanish School is well represented, from early masters

Martorell and Bermejo to the better-known names of the 16th and 17thC such as El Greco, Ribera, Zurbarán (see **A-Z**), Murillo (see **A-Z**) and Velázquez (see **A-Z**) and on to Goya, as well as important paintings by Seville artists whose work is not often seen outside Spain: Sánchez de Castro, Alejo Fernández, Juan de las Roelas, Valdés Leal (see **A-Z**) and the Herreras (Elder and Younger). See MUSEUMS.

Best Buys: Decorated earthenware plates, bowls, jugs and wall tiles feature high on the list of best buys. La Cartuja de Sevilla crockery sometimes uses English patterns, as the factory was founded by Englishman Charles Pickman last century. Other local handcrafted items are leather goods, silver-, gold- and ironwork, and embroidery. Traditional costumes and accessories include *sevillanas* (see **A-Z**) and flamenco outfits, capes and shawls, hair combs, painted fans and wide-brimmed hats. Spain's fashion designers have been gaining an international reputation and Seville has a good selection of shops selling their distinctive designs. Castanets, beautifully crafted guitars and records or cassettes of classical and flamenco performers are also good mementos. See CRAFTS, SHOPPING 1 & 2, Ceramics, Markets.

Bicycle & Motorcycle Hire: There are no official hire companies in Seville. The motor scooter (*moto* or *escúter*) is an extremely popular method of transport in Seville but it is not recommended for novices. Bicycles are not a common sight within the city itself, though cycling as a sport is extremely popular throughout Spain. Again, cycling is not recommended, except for the most experienced.

Budget:

Pensión (one night)	2000ptas
4-star hotel (one night)	4500ptas
Breakfast in bar (coffee & toast)	200ptas
Ración of seafood	500ptas
Glass of wine	75ptas
Bus fare	70ptas
Taxi across city	400ptas
Museum visit	250ptas

Bullfighting: The sport, as well as other rituals involving bulls, has been practised in Spain for thousands of years. Nowadays it has become an increasingly contentious issue among both foreigners and Spaniards. Nevertheless, its danger and excitement have often been elements of Spain's romantic appeal, and its erotic symbolism and the dance-like movements of the torero have attracted artists such as Goya and Picasso and writers such as Hemingway. Carmen in Bizet's opera was killed at Seville's bullring, La Maestranza. It was begun in 1761 and is one of Spain's oldest and biggest. There are corridas on Sun. evenings April-Oct. and daily during the Feria de Abril (see **A-Z**). Tickets for performances by the top toreros are often hard to obtain except from touts at inflated prices. Children under 15 are not admitted.

Buses: The city has a comprehensive bus network. Most routes pass through Pl. Nueva, Pl. de la Encarnación, Pl. del Duque or Pl. Magdalena. Within the centre it is usually quicker to walk, while the relatively inexpensive taxis (see **A-Z**) are quickest for journeys to other districts. The basic bus fare is 70ptas, although a *bonobus* (saver ticket) costing 390ptas is valid for 10 journeys. For information, tel: 4420011/ 4225360 or ask at the central office, c/ Diego de Riaño 2. Buses C1, C2, 40, 41 and 42 go to Triana. The last two also go to Los Remedios. Out-of-city bus services operate from the main terminal at c/ Manuel Vázquez Sagastizabal s/n, tel: 4417111. The service to Huelva operates from c/ Segura 16, tel: 4222272.

Cameras & Photography: All leading brand names and popular sizes of film are available. Keep film and cameras out of the heat. Do not attempt to photograph policemen, military personnel and installations. Photography, or use of flashlight, is not allowed in some buildings. Films, as well as developing and printing, are generally higher priced in Spain than in other European countries. A number of shops provide a fast developing and printing service.

Camping & Caravanning: There are four official categories from 1 to 3 and L (luxury). Off-site camping is not encouraged and it is not allowed on beaches, in mountain areas, along dry river beds, within 1 km of a town or 150 m of a drinking-water supply. Tinder-dry vegetation is a high fire hazard in summer. There are three camping sites close to Seville: Camping Sevilla, tel: 4514379, 6 km from the city on the N IV; Club de Campo, tel: 4513927, 12 km along the N IV; and Camping Wilson, tel: 4720828, 12.8 km along the N IV.

Car Hire: All the big international firms operate in the city, directly or with local associates. Small local firms, whose leaflets can be picked up at hotels and tourist offices, usually have lower rates. Scheduled airlines and holiday operators have car-hire offers. There are also firms which undertake bulk hiring so that they can pass on substantial discounts to tourists. Their leaflets may be available through the Spanish tourist board in your country. Your hotel may have a lower price arrangement too. Insurance and mileage charges may add considerably to the bill. Insurance should include third party and a bail bond. It is advisable to take comprehensive insurance including a collision damage waiver. VAT (IVA) is charged at 12%. See **Accidents & Breakdowns**, **Driving**.

Caridad, Hospital de la: The Hospital of Charity for the sick poor was set up by a lay brotherhood drawn from the noble classes in Seville. Other functions of the brotherhood included the burying of criminals and plague victims and today it runs the old people's home which now occupies the Hospital. The building dates from the 17thC when the head of the brotherhood was Miguel de Mañara, often thought to have been the model for Don Juan (see **A-Z**). The church is decorated on the exterior with ceramic panels. Inside are important paintings from the last major series by Murillo (see **A-Z**). These and the sculpture *The Entombment of Christ* on the magnificent Baroque (see **A-Z**) altarpiece highlight the charitable aims of the brotherhood. Its spiritual ones are spectacularly shown in Valdés Leal's (see **A-Z**) paintings of the triumph of death over material wealth. See **BUILDINGS 1**.

Cartuja, La: The 20thC 'island' of La Cartuja was created when the course of the Río Guadalquivir (see **A-Z**) was diverted away from the city to prevent further flooding. The site was then developed for the Expo '92 Universal Exhibition (see **A-Z**). The area takes its name from the Carthusian monastery, La Cartuja de Santa María de las Cuevas (see **BUILDINGS 2**), extensively restored to become the Royal Pavilion of Expo '92. The church and chapels, cloister and refectory remain of the monastery, begun in the 15thC in *mudéjar* (see **A-Z**) style, with subsequent Renaissance and Baroque (see **A-Z**) additions. Columbus (see **A-Z**) derived friendship and support from one of its monks, Fray Gaspar de Gorricio, and was temporarily buried here in the Chapel of Santa Ana. After the dissolution of the monasteries in the 19thC, the Englishman Charles Pickman established the Cartuja de Sevilla ceramics factory here (see **Ceramics**). The chimneys of its kilns are still prominent, though the factory has moved to a new site.

Casa de la Contratación: This was the controlling body set up in 1503 when Seville was granted the monopoly on Spanish trade with the Indies. It planned the twice-yearly fleets and had schools of navigation and map-making. The Sala de los Almirantes (Admirals' Hall) in the Reales Alcázares (see **BUILDINGS 1**) is all that remains of its building but its records are preserved in the Archivo General de las Indias (see

MUSEUMS). The city lost the monopoly to Cádiz in 1717, setting the seal on its decline as a port.

Catedral: 'Let us build a cathedral so huge that on seeing it people will think us madmen.' This was the resolution of the Cathedral Chapter in 1401. To carry it out, the site of the Grand Mosque was cleared, which in turn had replaced an early Visigothic (see **A-Z**) church. The new Cathedral was indeed the world's largest at the time, superseded later only by Rome's St. Peter's and London's St. Paul's. Later additions to the exterior make it difficult to appreciate the sheer mass and the spectacular flying buttresses of the Gothic (see **A-Z**) building, except from the top of the Giralda (see **BUILDINGS 1**). Inside, its great size is immediately apparent. Huge, more than 75 m wide and 100 m in length, its gloomy lighting heightens the atmosphere of

solemnity. There are five naves, supported on massive columns rising high to the vaulted ceiling. Numerous side chapels have a wealth of sculpture and paintings but the most breathtaking (and ostentatious) grandeur is reserved for the Capilla Mayor with its huge 18 m-high altarpiece of painted and gilded relief carvings. In the Capilla Real are the remains of the sainted King Fernando III (see **A-Z**), who captured Seville from the Moors (see **A-Z**), and the revered image of La Virgen de los Reyes (Virgin of the Kings). The Sacristía Mayor and Sacristía de los Cálices have paintings by many of the great masters of Spanish art, the keys of the city surrendered to

Fernando III in 1248 and the Cathedral's rich treasury of gold and silver. Near the tourists' entrance is the huge tomb of Columbus (see **A-Z**), erected here when his remains were brought back from Cuba in 1899. The delightful Moorish Patio de los Naranjos (see **Patios**), formerly the *sahn* (ablutions courtyard) of the mosque, opens off the north side. See **BUILDINGS 1**.

Catholic Monarchs: The two Spanish kingdoms of Castile and Aragón were united through the marriage of Isabel and Ferdinand in 1469. They dedicated themselves to the Christian Reconquest and Isabel set up the Inquisition. For their zeal in spreading and defending the faith they gained the title of the Catholic Monarchs from the Pope. In Seville, which already belonged to Castile, they made additions at the Reales Alcázares (see **BUILDINGS 1**), making it a base from which to plan the assault on the last Moorish stronghold, Granada, which they captured in 1492. That year Columbus (see **A-Z**) reached the Americas, while at home Jews (see **A-Z**) who refused to convert to Christianity were expelled. Moors (see **A-Z**) were also given the alternative of conversion or expulsion. Important communities of Jewish *conversos* and *moriscos* (see **A-Z**) remained in Seville.

Ceramics: *azulejos.* Ceramics have remained an important craft industry throughout Seville's history. The city has been known for pottery from Roman times, and Justa and Rufina (see **A-Z**), patron saints of Seville, were potters. Later, distinctive ceramic tiles, often with beautiful colour glazes and complex geometric patterns, became an integral feature of Seville's Moorish (see **A-Z**) and *mudéjar* (see **A-Z**) design. The best examples are in the 14thC Palace of King Pedro the Cruel at the Reales Alcázares (see **BUILDINGS 1**) and the 16thC Casa de Pilatos (see **BUILDINGS 1**). Examples of Spanish tin-glazed earthenware, Hispano-Moresque ware, often produced in Triana, became popular throughout Europe in the 19thC, while in the same century Charles Pickman arrived in Seville with English designs and set up La Cartuja (see **A-Z**) ceramics factory, still producing today and with a shop in c/ García Vinuesa. More traditional Spanish painted earthenware is still produced in Triana, where there are several factory shops. See **CRAFTS**, **Best Buys**.

Cervantes

Cervantes, Miguel de (1547-1616):

The creator of *Don Quixote* was for a time imprisoned in Seville for not paying his taxes. The prison, now disappeared, was on the corner of c/ Sierpes and Pl. de San Francisco. It is believed that he began his great work there, while his *Novelas Ejemplares* include references to 16thC Seville.

Charles V, Emperor (1516-56):

Much of Seville's expansion in the 16thC occurred under Emperor Charles V, the first of the Hapsburg rulers of Spain. Although Charles himself spent little time in Spain before his abdication to the Spanish monastery of Yuste in 1556, his marriage to Isabel of Portugal in 1526 took place in Seville's Reales Alcázares (see **BUILDINGS 1**), where the royal apartments were added to, introducing Renaissance style. The Ayuntamiento (see **BUILDINGS 1**), built during his reign, incorporates statues of him and his Empress on the facade. The Emperor's special device of two columns with the motto 'Plus ultra' ('More beyond'), which appears there and at the Alcázar, was particularly popular in Seville, the columns being interpreted as the Pillars of Hercules at the entrance to the Mediterranean and the motto to the discovery of the Americas beyond.

Charles III, King:

Although Seville's importance had declined by the 18thC, her links with the Indies were continued under the Bourbon Kings. In 1785 Charles III established the Archivo General de las Indias (see **MUSEUMS**) in Seville's 16thC trade exchange, while the imposing Fábrica de Tabacos (see **BUILDINGS 2**) for the lucrative state monopoly of tobacco was completed during his reign.

Chemists: Chemists (*farmacias*) have a green cross sign. A notice on the door will give the address of the nearest chemist open after normal hours. Prescription medicines are relatively inexpensive. Many medicines are available without prescription and chemists can offer valuable advice. First-aid preparations, patent medicines, insect repellents and condoms are also sold. See **Health**.

Children: As is customary in Mediterranean countries, children are made very welcome almost everywhere and at any time. Nevertheless, as Seville is a busy city with a great deal of sightseeing, parents may consider that visiting it would be more relaxing (and romantic) without the responsibility of caring for the needs of children. Recommendations for children include the museums and parks, the Giralda (see **BUILDINGS 1**), boat and horse-drawn carriage trips (see **A-Z**) and the funfair at the Parque de Atracciones (beyond Los Remedios district). Ask the tourist office for details of special children's events. See **Baby-sitters.**

Churches: Visitors to Seville's churches are requested to dress and behave with respect for their function as places of worship. Shorts are generally banned. Apart from the Cathedral, where there is a charge for a tourist visit, churches are free and are generally only open for Mass and other services. Half an hour before or after morning or evening Mass is usually a good time to visit, though visitors may often remain during services provided that they do not disturb worshippers. Machines taking 5 or 25ptas coins often provide lighting for side chapels. As well as those mentioned under **BUILDINGS** and **WALKS**, the following churches are also of interest: San Luis in the street of the same name, towards the Macarena Gate, the best example of a High Baroque (see **A-Z**) church in Seville; Santa Catalina, c/ Juan de Mesa, with a *mudéjar* (see **A-Z**) tower; the Capilla de Maese Rodrigo, Puerta de Jerez (turn left, end of Av de la Constitución), an early 16thC chapel once part of a university college founded by Rodrigo de Santaella; Iglesia de la Asunción, c/ Goyeneta, the church of the old university, with fine Renaissance tombs of the Enríquez Ribera family who built the Casa de Pilatos (see **BUILDINGS 1**), and a monument to the 19thC poet Gustavo Adolfo Bécquer.

Cinco Llagas, Hospital de las: The Hospital of the Five Wounds, also known as the Hospital de la Sangre (of the Blood). This extensive Renaissance building, begun in 1546 and situated just outside the city walls, was a charitable foundation funded by nobility which originally cared for women with incurable diseases and later for victims of plague. It continued to function as a hospital until the mid-1960s and has recently been converted to house the Andalusian parliament, with its debating chamber in the former hospital church.

Cinema: Spain has an active and adventurous film industry and an enthusiastic cinema-going population. Most foreign films are dubbed. Films in the original language with Spanish subtitles are advertised as 'v.o.' In summer there are open-air cinemas at the Parque de Atracciones and the Prado de San Sebastián.

Cita en Sevilla: A season of cultural events which follows the Feria de Abril (see **A-Z**) and continues into June. There are performances of opera, theatre, music and dance, as well as art exhibitions and street theatre. Posters and leaflets give details. See **Newspapers**, **What's On**.

City Walls: A much restored stretch of the city walls remains in the Macarena district. The battlemented walls with lookout towers date from the Moors' (see **A-Z**) strengthening of the fortifications around the 12thC, while the Puerta de la Macarena, the only remaining gateway, was rebuilt in the 16thC and extensively restored. The walls of the Alcázar gardens also formed part of the city walls and the present-day *ronda* (ring road) still follows their line.

Climate: Although the climate of Andalucía is generally classified as Mediterranean, Seville's inland situation causes more extremes of temperature. Average temperatures and rainfall during the seasons are: spring 27°C, 94 mm; summer 35°C, 34 mm; autumn 24°C, 140 mm; winter 18°C, 107mm. Summer temperatures can soar to 45°C and in winter it is seldom below 12°C. Hours of sunshine exceed 2800 a year. Spring and autumn are undoubtedly the most pleasant times for a visit.

Columbus, Christopher (1446-1506): Cristóbal Colón in Spanish. Of Genoese family (though his birthplace is still disputed), Christopher Columbus, joined by his brother, Diego, became cartographers in Portugal. There he first sought royal sponsorship for his mission to find a sea route to the East Indies. Support was also solicited from the English. Based at the monastery of La Rábida (1000-1300 Tue.-Sun.), near Palos de la Frontera, and aided by its prior, he pursued his aims with Spain's Catholic Monarchs (see **A-Z**), eventually meeting them in Córdoba and getting their blessing and financial support. In three small caravels, with the *Santa María* as his flagship, he set sail on 3 Aug. 1492 and made his first major landfall on 12 Oct. on the Caribbean island of San Salvador. He returned to Spain the following year to make his report to the Catholic Monarchs. Subsequently he made two more voyages to the Caribbean, having been appointed Viceroy there. For 27 years his body was interred at the monastery of La Cartuja (see **BUILDINGS 2**) with whose monks Columbus and his family had long maintained a close association. Afterwards his remains were taken to Cuba and returned to Seville only in the 19thC, when his monumental tomb in the Catedral (see **BUILDINGS 1**) was erected. He is also commemorated in Seville by a monument in the Jardines de Catalina de Ribera (see **WALK 4**). Charts and other documents of his can be seen in the Archivo General de las Indias (see **MUSEUMS**). The selection of Seville to host Expo '92 (see **A-Z**), as well as its site and theme, was partly to commemorate 1992, the quincentenary of Columbus' first voyage to America.

Complaints: Hotels, tourist apartments, camp sites, restaurants and petrol stations are required by law to keep *hojas de reclamación* (complaint forms) in triplicate. If your complaint is about price, you must first pay the bill before requesting the forms. One copy is retained by you, another is sent to the tourism department of the regional government and the third is kept by the establishment against which the complaint is being made. Your local tourist office may advise if you need help in translating the form (see **Tourist Information**).

Consulates: Some 35 countries have consulates in Seville and 1992 sees the opening of many more in the city. For those not listed here, telephone directories give their addresses and telephone numbers.
UK – Pl. Nueva 8, tel: 4228875.
Canada – Av de la Constitución 30, tel: 4229413.
USA – Pabellón EEUU, Paseo de las Delicias 7, tel: 4231885.

Convents: Note that in Spanish the word *convento* can mean either a convent or a monastery. Seville has many of both, some of them set up or enlarged during the 16thC to train monks and nuns bound for the Indies. Many of the convents are notable for their art and architecture, though a number belonging to closed orders of nuns can only be viewed from the outside. The Convento de Santa Paula, c/ Santa Paula 11, combines Gothic (see **A-Z**), *mudéjar* (see **A-Z**) and Renaissance elements, and has an attractive cloister and a small museum. The nuns also sell jams, Seville orange marmalades and bitter orange sweets. The Convento de Santa Inés, c/ Doña María Coronel, is a Gothic and *mudéjar* building in which María Coronel sought refuge from the attentions of King Pedro the Cruel after disfiguring her face with burning oil. Her body is preserved in the convent. Images of her and sweets can be bought at the revolving window. Another beautiful convent with

Gothic, *mudéjar* and later elements is Santa Clara, c/ Santa Ana 40 (open only during early-morning Mass), entered through a delightful patio (see **A-Z**) which also leads to the 13thC Tower of Don Fadrique.

Conversion Chart:

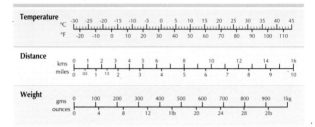

Corpus Christi: During Corpus Christi at the end of May, rosemary, sage and rose petals cover many of Seville's streets and palm branches are hung from balconies. A procession, of which a huge silver *custodia* containing the Host is the centrepiece, moves from the Cathedral to Pl. de San Francisco and back again. In Triana the following day there are similar processions called Corpus Chico. See **Seises**.

Costa de la Luz: The nearest beaches to Seville. The *costa* comprises two sections, from Huelva province to Cádiz, and south of Cádiz to Tarifa, continental Europe's most southerly point. The coastline is characterized by wide, open beaches of fine sand and development has been more restrained than on most of Spain's coast. Resorts include Mazagón, with the Parador Cristóbal Colón nearby; Matalascañas, a modern purpose-built resort; Puerto de Santa María, a sherry port with resort facilities and lively nightlife; and the delightful port of Sanlúcar de Barrameda where manzanilla, similar to fino sherry, is made.

Coto de Doñana Nature Reserve: Southwest of Seville, between the main course of the Río Guadalquivir (see **A-Z**) and the Atlantic Costa de la Luz (see **A-Z**), is the 75,000 hectare Coto de Doñana Nature Reserve. Its unique ecosystem of marshland, sand dunes and scrub supports a huge population of birds, including flamingos and many migratory species, and mammals such as wild boar, deer, lynx and mongoose. A free tour of a limited area starts from the entrance just beyond El Rocío (see **Rocío**) (0800 Tue.-Sun., tel: 955-406140), while longer, guided tours in Land Rovers start from El Acebùche, 5 km from the coast (1500 Tue.-Sun.; 1600ptas, advanced booking necessary, tel: 955-430432). For further information contact the World Wide Fund for Nature, Ave du Mont Blanc 1196, Gland, Switzerland.

Credit Cards: See **Money**.

Crime & Theft: Like many cities, Seville has in recent years unfortu-nately gained a reputation for crime against tourists. People in holiday mood can be prime targets for bag snatchers, pickpockets and thieves who break into cars and accommodation. Some advice: deposit your valuables in the hotel safe; carry the least possible amount of cash; take care about flashing cash around and when leaving a bank; carry hand-bags with shoulder straps across your body and the bag on the off-street side (best, don't carry them at all); keep cameras hidden when not in use; don't wear jewellery; avoid lonely places; don't leave anything in sight in a car; use taxis late at night; don't try to be heroic. If you have been the subject of a crime, try to find witnesses and report the incident to the police immediately. Make sure to get a copy of your statement for insurance purposes. See **Consulates**, **Emergency Numbers**, **Insurance**, **Police**.

Currency: The peseta (pta) is Spain's monetary unit. Notes: 10,000; 5000; 2000; 1000; 500 (going out of circulation). Coins: 500; 200; 100; 50; 25; 5; 1. See **Money**.

Customs Allowances:

Duty Paid Into:	Cigarettes	or	Cigars	or	Tobacco	Spirits	Wine
E C	300		75		400 g	1.5 l	5 l
U K	300		75		400 g	1.5 l	5 l

Dentists: See **Health**.

Disabled Travellers: Unfortunately, as in many countries, special amenities are all too few and so it is advisable to inform travel agents or holiday operators of specific needs before confirming bookings. One frequent provision is of public telephone kiosks for wheelchair users. Although not specially adapted, the Cathedral, Reales Alcázares and Casa de Pilatos have reasonable wheelchair access. See **Insurance**.

Don Juan: The Spanish dramatist Tirso de Molina (1584-1648) first created the character of Don Juan Tenorio, the scoundrel lover of Seville and exploiter of women's emotions. In literature the character was also taken up by Molière in French, Zorrilla again in Spanish and Byron in English and perhaps most famously by Mozart in his opera. The model for the character was often thought to have been the real-life 17thC Sevillian, Don Miguel de Mañara, who became head of the Hospital de la Caridad (see **BUILDINGS 1**), though he was an infant when Tirso's work first appeared! A statue of the mythical figure stands in the Pl. de Refinadores, Barrio de Santa Cruz.

Drinks: *Agua potable* (*del grifo*), drinking (tap) water, although safe may have some unwanted effects simply because your system is not used to it. It's best to stick to *agua mineral*, *con gas* or *sin gas*, bottled mineral water, still or carbonated. *Té*, tea, is usually served with a slice of lemon. *Infusión de manzanilla* is camomile tea. *Horchata* is a cool, refreshing drink made from groundnuts. *Granizado* is iced, fresh fruit juice. Coffee is served as *café solo* (black), *con leche* (with milk), *cortado* (with a spot of milk), *americano* (with added water) and *descafeinado* (decaffeinated). *Chocolate*, thick hot chocolate, is served for breakfast or as a nightcap. Various local and imported beers, *cerveza*, are available. *Una caña*, draught beer, is usually lower priced. *Sangría*, a mixture of unknown potency, is made from red wine, brandy, soda, fruit juices and ice. See **Sherry**, **Wine**.

Driving: There is heavy traffic congestion in Seville at peak times. Many of its streets are narrow and winding, often with one-way systems, so that visiting drivers may easily lose their bearings. Parking can also be difficult in the centre. Some problems have been alleviated by a new motorway around the town centre. At peak times, the *ronda* (ring road) is often quicker than crossing the city.

If you are taking your own car to Spain, take out good insurance and consult a motoring organization in your country for advice on procedures in the event of accident, theft or breakdown. If these happen in a hired car, contact the hire company for instructions.

You need the following with you when driving in Spain: passport, current driving licence (international or EC), vehicle registration document, third party insurance document and bail bond (usually covered by car-hire agreement document), spare headlight, sidelight and rearlight bulbs, red warning triangle (if you're going on motorways). The minimum driving age is 18. Drive on the right. A solid white line means no

overtaking or turning left. Speed limits are: 60 kph most urban roads; 90 kph other roads where indicated; 100 kph main roads; 120 kph motorways. Road signs follow international symbols. Belts must be worn in front seats outside urban areas. Don't drink and drive (permitted maximum is 0.8 g alcohol per 1000 cc). Penalties for this can be severe and include prison terms. See **Accidents & Breakdowns**, **Car Hire**, **Parking**, **Petrol**.

Drugs: Possession of small amounts of both soft and hard drugs for personal use remains legal within Spain but as amounts are not defined by law, possession of any drugs is a high risk. Trading in and importing drugs is illegal and suspects often spend months in prison awaiting trial. Convicted traders and importers face harsh penalties.

Dueñas, Palacio de las: c/ Dueñas s/n. The residence of the Duke and Duchess of Alba may be visited by prior arrangement, tel: 4220956

Plaza de España

or enquire at the tourist office. The Palacio, begun in the 15thC, has a beautiful arcaded patio (see **A-Z**) with *mudéjar* (see **A-Z**) plasterwork, and fine furniture and art.

Eating Out: Sevillians love eating out and the city has a wide choice of restaurants in every price bracket offering international cuisine, Andalusian and other Spanish regional specialities. Vegetarians, however, are not yet well catered for. Eating *tapas* (see **A-Z**) at Seville's many bars, dining at an open-air *terraza* and enjoying freshly-fried fish at one of its unpretentious *freidurías* are important Sevillian culinary experiences. The official grading of restaurants, 1 to 5 forks, reflects the standards of facilities, not that of the cooking. Price indications in the **RESTAURANTS** topic section refer to the price of main courses: Inexpensive, up to 1000ptas; Moderate, up to 2000ptas; Expensive, over 3000ptas. See **RESTAURANTS 1 & 2, TAPAS BARS, Food**.

Electricity: 220 or 225 V is now standard, although some old buildings occasionally still have 110 V and need a convertor for 220 V appliances. Some hotels provide 110 V sockets for shavers. Plugs are round pin with two points. Adaptors are available at most airports.

Emergency Numbers: Tel: 091 for the Policía Nacional. Concentrate on giving your location, the nature of the emergency and stating what other services may be required. See **Police**.

España, Plaza de: Aníbal González was the architect of this and some of the other buildings erected for the 1929 Ibero-American Exhibition. The massive semicircular building in *neo-mudéjar* (see **Mudéjar**) style is partly based on the 14thC Palace of Pedro the Cruel at the Reales Alcázares (see **BUILDINGS 1**). Below the arcade, the painted tiles depict Spain's 50 provinces. See **BUILDINGS 2**.

Events:
5 January: Cabalgata de los Reyes, processions of colourful floats from which the Three Kings rain sweets upon the crowd.
February: Carnaval, fancy dress parades, bands and choirs.

May: Cruces de Mayo, flower-covered patios and plazas and processions of children with paper-decorated crosses.

July: Velada de Santiago y Santa Ana, a centuries-old Triana festival, with dancing and merrymaking in c/ del Betis and Pl. del Altozano.

September (every second year): Bienal de Flamenco, a flamenco (see **A-Z**) festival with top performers.

8 December: La Inmaculada, celebrating the Immaculate Conception of the Virgin, when boys (see **Seises**) dance in the Cathedral.

See **Cita en Sevilla**, **Corpus Christi**, **Feria de Abril**, **Rocío**, **Semana Santa**.

Excursions: For information about city coach tours and beyond, pick up leaflets or enquire at your hotel, a travel agency or tourist office, or contact Compartecoche SA, c/ Amparo 22, tel: 4215494. Several companies, such as Sevillana de Cruceros, tel: 4211396, run boat excursions on the Río Guadalquivir. Their leaflets are available at hotels and tourist offices. Boats depart from Paseo Alcalde Marqués de Contadero, near the Torre del Oro. See **Horse-drawn Carriages**.

Expo '92: Opening on 20 April 1992, the Universal Exhibition of Seville 1992 (Expo '92) is the largest, most ambitious Universal Exhibition ever planned. Participants include some 100 countries, 20 international bodies, Spain's 17 autonomous communities and 20 international corporations. Its 215 hectare site on the Recinto de la Cartuja (see **Cartuja**) has more than half a million sq m of buildings, made up of more than 100 pavilions, 16 entertainment areas, 105 restaurants and 50 shops. The buildings are of spectacular, futuristic design, incorporating the most advanced materials and technologies. Both the British and the Danish pavilions feature flowing water to keep down the summer heat. Six new bridges across the Río Guadalquivir provide access and the site can be reached by car, bus, train, boat, helicopter, horse-drawn carriage and on foot. Transport within the site itself includes an elevated monorail, a cable car system, a water transportation network and 30 km of service roads. Almost half a million trees and plants of 400 different species and 35 km of hedges are being planted to create a microclimate in which high summer temperature should be reduced by 8°C. Seville and La Cartuja are appropriate for the Expo theme, 'The Age of Discovery' (see **A-Z**), in the year which celebrates the 500th anniversary of the first voyage of Columbus (see **A-Z**) to America, but the exhibition also explores the present and the future. More than 37 million visitors are expected before the exhibition closes on 12 Oct. 1992. After Expo '92 the site becomes a commercial, academic, scientific and technological complex.

Fábrica de Tabacos: Completed in 1771 and built around two large patios (see **A-Z**), it is Spain's second-largest building after the royal monastery-palace of El Escorial near Madrid. Its size reflects the economic importance of the state's monopoly on tobacco and Seville's continuing trading links with the Americas in the 18thC. As many as 10,000 women (*las cigarreras*) were employed rolling cigars. Stories of their doubtful morality were romanticized and epitomized in Bizet's *Carmen*. The building now houses Seville University. See **BUILDINGS 2**.

Feria de Abril: Just after the spectacular religious celebrations at Easter, the week-long Feria begins, one of the world's most exuberant festivals of Spring. The dates vary but there is generally one clear week between Easter and the April Fair. Beyond Los Remedios district are the Real de la Feria grounds, where *casetas,* striped tents, are erected by families, groups of friends, businesses, cultural groups and official organizations. Inside the *casetas* there is much eating and drinking, music and dancing of *sevillanas* (see **A-Z**). Access to the private *casetas* is by invitation only but many, such as those of the various districts of the city and the political parties, are open to the public. During the day there are colourful horseback processions from the city out to the fairground. In the afternoons, La Maestranza (see **Bullfighting**) draws crowds to the corridas where Spain's best bullfighters perform. At night, it's back to the fairground where the fun continues till dawn. Traditional costume is *andaluz* riding gear for men and tiered *sevillanas* dresses for women. The prices of many services and goods are raised during the period of the Feria and shops and banks have limited opening hours. Some roads are closed and there are special bus services to the fairground. Accommodation in the city and surrounding towns has to be reserved many months in advance.

Fernando III, 'el Santo' (1217-52): Ferdinand III, 'the Saint'. One of the patron saints of Seville. The Christian kingdoms of Castile and León were united through him, strengthening the Christian position in the Peninsula at a time when the Moors (see **A-Z**) were split into small, feuding territories. He led successful campaigns against the Moors, regaining much territory for Christianity, including Córdoba in

1236 and, in 1248, Seville, where he set up his Court. His silver tomb is in the Capilla Real of the Catedral (see **A-Z**) and his embalmed body is displayed to the public three times a year. He was canonized in the 17thC.

Flamenco: Much of what has been written about flamenco, particularly by foreigners, is misleadingly over-romantic. Current theories of its origins point to Indian influence brought by the gypsies. The most basic elements of flamenco are singing (*el cante*) and rhythm (*el compás*). Guitarists and dancers follow the singer, although the guitar and the dance, originally only accompaniments to the song, have gradually gained more importance. Popular forms of songs such as *soleares*,

alegrías and *bulerías*, have complex rhythms counted in twelves. To be out of time is the worst sin. The most serious and passionate form of flamenco is *cante jondo* (deep song). Another term frequently used by writers on flamenco is *duende*, when a piece is performed so passionately that the performer seems possessed. Both *cante jondo* and *duende* are by definition spontaneous, and a theatre or *tablao* is unlikely to create the right conditions. Instead of looking for the 'pure' flamenco advertised by all the *tablaos de flamenco*, it may be more realistic to look for performances of professional quality. As well as the *tablaos de flamenco* shows, there are also flamenco festivals (see **Events**) which attract top performers and touring companies which perform flamenco drama of the type popularized by Antonio Gades in films such as *Carmen*.

Food: In Seville, the main meal of the day is lunch, while dinner, unless at a restaurant, is usually a much lighter meal. Andalucía has a very varied cuisine, though olive oil, garlic and the benefit of extremely fresh produce are strong common denominators. Some typical dishes which visitors to Seville might try are: *gazpacho*, a cold soup of salad vegetables; *ensalada de Sevilla*, escolar, tarragon and olives; *huevos a la flamenca*, baked eggs, ham, spicy sausage, beans, peas, onions, garlic and tomato; *tortilla*, Spanish omelette with potato and other fillings; *rabo de toro*, bull's tail, often served with hot pepper, *picante guindilla*; *el menudo* or *callos a la andaluza*, a tripe stew; *ternera a la sevillana*, beef and olives cooked with white wine; *pato a la sevillana*, duck with bacon, peppers and olives. *Pescado frito*, fresh fish fried in very hot olive oil, is a true Andalusian speciality. Other fish include *salmonete* (red mullet), *pez espada* (swordfish) and *boquerones* (fresh anchovies), a favourite *tapa*. *Calamares* (squid) and *pulpo* (octopus) are also popular, as are *gambas* (prawns) and all types of shellfish such as *mejillones* (mussels) and *almejas* (cockles). There is always an abundance of fresh fruit. Of cheeses, *queso de Grazalema*, made from sheep's milk, is recommended. Traditional sweet biscuits include *torrijas*, made from bread and milk and sweetened with honey; *tortas de aceite*, flat cakes; and *polvorones*, shortcake biscuits. See **RESTAURANTS 1 & 2**, **TAPAS BARS**, **Eating Out**, **Tapas**.

Giralda: In 1184, the Almohade (see **A-Z**) Emir Abu Yusuf ordered the construction of the beautiful minaret for Seville's Grand Mosque. The Giralda was completed in 1198. In the 1560s the bell tower, which has 24 bells, and the upper storeys in a Tuscan Renaissance style were added. The Giraldilla weathervane is a bronze figure representing Faith some 100 m above ground level. Inside the tower is a ramp giving access to the top and magnificent views over the city. See **BUILDINGS 1**.

Golden Age: See **Siglo de Oro**.

Gothic: The architectural style dominant in Europe from the 12th-15thC. Its most easily recognized feature is the pointed arch, though others may include rib vaults, delicate tracery and, on the exterior of many churches, flying buttresses. It made its way into Spain from France and moved south with the Christian Reconquest. In Seville, its greatest expression is the Catedral (see **BUILDINGS 1**), the world's biggest

in the Gothic style. The harmonious combination of Gothic and *mudéjar* (see **A-Z**) elements, such as in the Iglesia de Santa Ana (see **BUILDINGS 2**) and at several convents (see **A-Z**), is uniquely Spanish.

Guadalquivir, Río: The name means 'great river' in Arabic. It runs for 657 km from the mountains of Cazorla (Jaén province) to its marshland estuary, Las Marismas, south of Seville. Once navigable as far as Córdoba, it is so nowadays only as far as Seville, Spain's only inland port. Today, the 'river' flowing through Seville is the Canal Alfonso XIII, constructed earlier this century, when the main course of the river was diverted around the city. Similarly, the creation of La Cartuja island (see **A-Z**) in the mid-1970s continued the work to protect Seville from regular and extensive flooding. The river is popular with water-sports enthusiasts throughout the year and there are regular regattas. The Club Náutico de Sevilla has private mooring and other facilities on the west bank near the Alfonso XIII bridge. See **Sports**.

Río Guadalquivir

Guides: Contact local tourist offices (see **Tourist Information**) for advice about the services of guides and interpreters, or write to: International Affairs Department, Patronato Provincial de Turismo de Sevilla, c/ Adolfo Rodríguez Jurado 2, 41001 Seville.

Health: Too much alcohol and too many late nights may take their toll on tourists. Pace your indulgence and your exposure to the sun. Drink bottled water and avoid ice. If your digestion is feeling the strain, eat simple vegetable dishes, omelettes, chicken or plain grilled fish. Health foods are available from *herboristerías*. Adequate travel insurance with accident and medical cover is advisable. Take a copy of the policy with you and make a separate note of its details and any emergency telephone numbers. Your hotel or *pensión* will assist in calling a doctor or making appointments with doctors or dentists. Tourist offices (see **Tourist Information**) and your consulate can provide lists of medical practitioners. You will be required to pay for each visit or consultation. Emergency cases are usually accepted at both public and private clinics or hospitals. Unless you have obtained a card entitling you to Spanish public health services (from DSS offices in Britain), you will be charged for these services. On presentation of your insurance policy, practitioners and clinics may agree to wait for payment of large bills from the insurers. See **Chemists**, **Emergency Numbers**, **Insurance**.

Hercules: It is part of Sevillian mythology that Hercules founded the city. He is commemorated by a statue on the facade of the Ayuntamiento (see **BUILDINGS 1**), as is Julius Caesar, who made Seville an assize town. They appear together again as 16thC statues on two columns in the Alameda de Hércules (see **WALK 2**). The columns are thought to have come from the Roman site at Itálica (see **EXCURSION 1**).

Horse-drawn Carriages: A romantic way of getting to know Seville is to hire a carriage. The driver will usually give a personal and extremely anecdotal explanation of the sights, mostly in Spanish. The price per hour is around 2000ptas. There are a number of ranks: in front of the Catedral, near the Torre del Oro, at Pl. de España and at the Jardines de Murillo. See **Excursions**.

Plaza de España

Insurance: Make sure you obtain adequate travel insurance which provides cover against theft, loss of property and medical expenses for the duration of your holiday. Your travel agent will be able to arrange this for you. See **Crime & Theft**, **Driving**, **Health**.

Jews: After the Christian Reconquest, Jews were allocated their enclosed *judería* (Jewish quarter) close to the Alcázar. Their contribution to scholarship and commerce was recognized by the Christian monarchy, whose protection permitted Jews to practice their religion and carry out their trades. The original *judería* extended from the Alcázar across the present-day *barrios* of Santa Cruz (see **WALK 1**) and San Bartolomé (see **WALK 2**). One of their synagogues (now the Church of Santa María la Blanca), many moneychangers' shops and their *azcuica* (market) stood on today's c/ Santa María la Blanca. In 1492, the Catholic Monarchs (see **A-Z**) ordered the expulsion of some 200,000 Jews from Spain and the enforced conversion of around 300,000.

Justa & Rufina: Two of the patron saints of Seville. In the 3rdC AD, these two Christian sisters, daughters of a potter from Triana, were imprisoned and later killed for refusing to worship Roman idols. In art they are usually shown with pots, the palms of martyrs and holding the Giralda tower, an anachronistic symbol of the city's Christian faith.

Language: The people of Andalucía speak Castilian Spanish. They have a different accent, of which the most notable feature is the pronunciation of the 'th' sound, as in the words 'Andalucía' and 'Jerez', as 's'. They also tend to clip endings off some words, for example 'demasiado' (too much) becomes 'demasiao' and 'para' (for) becomes 'pa'.

Laundries: Hotels have laundry and dry-cleaning services. A *lavandería* (Launderette) or a *tintorería* (dry cleaner) will usually be cheaper. They charge by weight and need a minimum of 24 hr.

Lebrija, Palacio de la Condesa de: The residence of the Countess of Lebrija may be visited by prior arrangement, tel: 4227802 or enquire at the tourist office (see **Tourist Information**). The Palacio at c/ Cuna 18 has examples of fine *mudéjar* (see **A-Z**) work but its prize feature is a large Roman mosaic from Itálica (see **EXCURSION 1**) which covers the central patio (see **A-Z**). Also on show are sculptures, ceramics, glass and other artefacts spanning Iberian, Roman and Moorish periods.

Lost Property: Any losses in a hotel or *pensión* should be reported first to the hall porter or person in charge, who will take details and investigate. The lost property office is at c/ Almansa 21 and is open weekday mornings. Some form of identification is needed. If the loss is serious, report it to the Policía Nacional (see **Police**). Promptly advise credit card companies, issuers of traveller's cheques and, if your passport is lost, your consulate (see **A-Z**). See **Insurance**.

Macarena, La: This Baroque (see **A-Z**) sculpture of the Virgin is sometimes attributed to the Seville sculptress Luisa Roldán (see **Sculpture**). One of several images of Our Lady of Hope which appear in the Holy Week processions, La Macarena is the most passionately revered. She is kept in the Basílica de la Macarena (0900-1300, 1700-2100), built during the 1940s near the Macarena Gate and the City Walls (see **A-Z**) in the northeast of the city. Her wealth of jewels and treasure is displayed in the Museum (0930-1230, 1730-1930; 100ptas). Her procession to the Cathedral on Good Fri. is one of the high points of Holy Week. See **Semana Santa**.

Markets: A lively market takes place at the Alameda de Hércules (0900-1500 Sun.). Stalls sell crafts, jewellery, gift items and second-hand merchandise and antiques of variable quality. The Sun. morning Triana market in c/ San Martín de Porres is also popular. Also on Sun. there is a coin and stamp market in the Pl. del Cabildo and a market for birds and other domestic pets in Pl. Alfalfa. El Mercado del Jueves, a flea-market selling almost every kind of old and used item, is held in c/ Feria on Thu. until 1500. Murillo (see **A-Z**) is said to have begun his career selling his paintings here! Throughout the week there are stalls selling crafts and jewellery in Pl. del Duque. There is a large indoor market for fresh produce in Pl. de la Encarnación, open 7 days. See **Best Buys**, **Shopping**.

Money: Banks offer the best exchange rate. Your passport is needed for any transaction. The major international credit and charge cards are widely accepted, as are traveller's cheques in any western European currency or US dollars. A number of Spanish banks are wary of Eurocheques, even when supported by a valid card. You may be able to use your credit and charge cards at some cash dispensers in Spain. Check with the company before you go. See **Currency**.

Moorish: The Moors' (see **A–Z**) legacy of architecture and decoration in Spain gives an exotic and distinctly non-European look to much of Andalucía. Most easily recognized are the horseshoe arches. Characteristics of the caliphate style at Córdoba (see **EXCURSION 2**) include complex vaulting and rich surface decoration, as in the Mezquita. The stricter Almohades (see **A–Z**) insisted on areas of repose for the eye, hence the delicate brickwork in trellis patterns on the Giralda (see **BUILDINGS 1**) in Seville.

Mezquita

Moors: The collective word describing the Muslim tribes of Arabs, Syrians, Berbers and others who invaded the Iberian Peninsula from North Africa in AD 711. The Moors' invasion was aided by the Visigoth (see **A-Z**) Archbishop Oppa of Seville who connived with the Moors' leader, Tarik, whose forces overran the Visigoths at a battle on the banks of the Río Guadalete. Seville was conquered the following year. The Moors' domination of the Peninsula was consolidated in AD 756, when Abderraman, a descendant of the Muslim dynasty in Damascus, declared himself an independent Emir with Córdoba (see **EXCURSION 2**) as his capital. In AD 929 Abderraman III established the independent caliphate of Córdoba, ushering in the most united, progressive and scholarly period of Moorish rule in the Peninsula. The caliphate ended with the abdication of Hisham III in 1031, when the Moorish territories split into *taifas* (small kingdoms) and the Reconquest thereafter began to gain ground. See **Almohades**.

Moriscos: Muslims who converted to Christianity.

Mudéjar: A Muslim under Christian rule. The term is usually applied to the Moorish (see **A-Z**) style and techniques in architecture and decoration which continued and developed in Christianized Spain from the 13th-16thC, or to the Muslim craftsmen who carried out such work. Features include plasterwork with intricate patterns often based on Arabic script, geometric-design tiles (*azulejos*) and distinctive ceilings which range from *artesonado* (wooden coffering) to spectacular honeycombed domes. *Mudéjar* frequently combined with the more familiarly European styles of Gothic (see **A-Z**) and Renaissance and there were even echoes of it in Baroque (see **A-Z**). This century the style has been revived in Seville as *neo-mudéjar*, notably in the buildings for the 1929 Ibero-American Exhibition (see **España**).

Murillo, Bartolomé Esteban (1617-82): One of the most important Spanish painters of the 17thC and perhaps Seville's best-loved son, even today. His compositions introduced a new naturalism which made religious subjects more accessible and his mature style had none of the stark light and shade contrasts often associated with

Spanish painting. As well as religious works, which included many of the Immaculate Conception of the Virgin, other subjects included street urchins and some fine portraits. Examples of his work may be seen in the Museo de Bellas Artes (see **MUSEUMS**), Catedral (see **BUILDINGS 1**) and Hospital de la Caridad (see **BUILDINGS 1**), as well as other churches and convents and the Museo-Casa de Murillo (see **MUSEUMS**, **WALK 1**).

Newspapers: *El País*, Spain's most widely respected daily newspaper, publishes an Andalusian edition. *ABC*, *El Correo de Andalucía* and *Diario de Andalucía* are other dailies published in Seville. All have listings of events in the city. *Cambalache* is a weekly classified advertisements magazine. Many European and American newspapers and magazines are available at higher prices than in their home countries. Some foreign newspapers are available on their day of publication. There are also weekly digests from the English-language newspapers. See **What's On**.

Nightlife: After dinner, about 2230, nightlife begins. Lively areas are near the Cathedral, around Pl. Daoiz and Pl. Alfalfa and along Av de la Constitución, the Barrio de Santa Cruz and Triana. Much of the later nightlife, from about 0100, is in modern Los Remedios, where music bars and discos are often open till 0400 or even later. The city's red-light district around the Alameda de Hércules is extremely seedy and can be dangerous. See **NIGHTLIFE 1 & 2**, **RESTAURANTS 1 & 2**, **TAPAS BARS**.

NO8DO: The condensed form of the motto of Seville – *No me ha dejado* (It has not deserted me) – a reference to the city's support for King Fernando III (see **A-Z**) who captured the city from the Moors (see **A-Z**) in 1248. *Nodo* means 'knot' in Spanish, represented by the 8. The device appears on many buildings, including the Ayuntamiento (see **BUILDINGS 1**), on the buses and even on manhole covers.

Opening times: In general:
Banks – 0900-1400 Mon.-Fri., 0900-1300 Sat.
Government offices – 1100-1300 Mon.-Fri. (for public business).
Main post office – 0900-1300, 1700-1900 Mon.-Fri., 0900-1400 Sat.

Restaurants – breakfast until 1100; lunch 1400-1600; dinner 2100 on.
Shops – All are open 1000-1300, 1700-1900 Mon.-Fri. Some are open
on Sat. evening and department stores stay open till 2100 Mon.-Sat.
Museums, etc. – Only summer times (May-Sep.) are given in this guide.
In winter, attractions often open later and close earlier. Times are cor-
rect at time of going to press but tourist offices do monthly updates.

Orientation: Seville is situated 8 m above sea level, some 115 km
inland from the sea along the navigable Río Guadalquivir (see **A-Z**). It
is divided into 24 *barrios* (districts). The main city is on the left (east)
bank of the river. Triana and Los Remedios districts are on the opposite
bank, reached by the principal bridge, Puente de San Telmo, and others. The Recinto de la Cartuja (see **Cartuja**) is also on the west bank. A
good map of Seville is particularly helpful for finding your way in the
winding central streets. Free maps are available from tourist offices and
at most hotels. More detailed ones can be bought at kiosks, bookshops
and some tobacconists. Detailed maps of the region, available from
bookshops, are advisable for planning excursions beyond the city.
There have been extensive changes to both city and regional road systems so check the publication date. See CITY DISTRICTS, **Andalucía**.

Palacio de Congresos y Exposiciones: Seville's modern conference and exhibition centre is located in the Polígono Aeropuerto district on the N IV highway east of the city. Its four buildings comprise
165,000 sq m, and the main conference hall has a capacity of 1300
people. All modern facilities and services are available.

Palacios: Seville has numerous grand houses. Many were built during the period of Seville's great wealth derived from having the
monopoly of trade with the Americas. The traditional Andalusian elements of interior patios (see **A-Z**) and *mudéjar* (see **A-Z**) decoration
were often combined with other styles, such as Gothic (see **A-Z**) and
Renaissance. A number of good 16thC merchants' *palacios* survive
around c/ Abades (see **WALK 2**), while the Av de las Palmeras has
impressive *palacios* dating from earlier this century, many of them originally pavilions for the 1929 exhibition. See **Dueñas**, **Lebrija**, **Pilatos**.

Paradores Nacionales: These are the hotels of a state-sponsored organization. Though expensive, they offer value for money and many are superbly sited in magnificent old buildings. Seville itself has no *parador*. The nearest are at Santiponce (8 km) (see **EXCURSION 1**) and Carmona (38 km) (see **EXCURSION 2**). There is a central booking office in Madrid, tel: 91-4359700.

Parking: Parking is very difficult in the centre of Seville. There are underground car parks at Pl. Nueva and Pl. Gavidia. The Policía Municipal do enforce parking regulations, so be aware of restrictions, usually clearly marked by signs and painted lines on the kerb. See **Driving**.

Passports & Customs: Visitors holding a valid passport of an EC country or of the United States and Canada do not require a visa to enter Spain for a stay not exceeding 90 days. British visitors' passports are also accepted. Australian, New Zealand, South African, Japanese and some other passport holders have to obtain a visa from a Spanish consulate in their country of permanent residence. See **Customs Allowances**.

Patios: These are a distinctive and practical feature of Andalusian buildings, both domestic and public. The tradition of cool interior courtyards was common to both the Moors (see **A-Z**) and the Jews (see **A-Z**) in Seville. Traditional patios provide delightful summer living spaces; they are generally decorated with *azulejos* (tiles) and fragrant plants, and some even have fountains. Those at the Reales Alcázares (see **BUILDINGS 1**) and Casa de Pilatos (see **BUILDINGS 1**) are particularly spectacular but typical ones can be spied through doorways all over Seville. There are two public patios which still provide welcome shade and quiet in the heart of the busy city: the Patio de los Naranjos (Courtyard of Orange Trees), originally the ablutions courtyard of the mosque, now the Cathedral cloister and reached through the Catedral (see **A-Z**) or viewed from the attractive Puerta del Perdón; and the Patio de Banderas, also filled with orange trees, one of the entrances to the Jewish quarter.

Peninsular War (1808-14): Napoleon's troops entered the Peninsula in 1808 after the abdication of King Charles IV. Spanish, Portuguese and British forces eventually defeated the French and the Spanish Bourbon monarchy was restored. Seville was occupied by the French Marischal Soult, who removed a number of important paintings for his own collection, including some by Murillo (see **A-Z**) from the Hospital de la Caridad (see **BUILDINGS 1**).

Petrol: Petrol (*gasolina*) is available in *normal* (2 star, 90 octane), *súper* (4 star, 96 octane) and *extra* (98 octane) grades, as well as *sin plomo* (unleaded). Diesel is *gas-oil*. There are petrol stations along all main routes into and out of the city and many are open 24 hr. Outside the city on minor roads they are infrequent except at towns and are generally open 0800-1500, 1600-2000 Mon.-Sat. See **Driving**.

Philip II (1556-98): Son of Emperor Charles V (see **A-Z**), Philip was given Spain and its dominions in the division of the Hapsburg Empire. Seville's pivotal position controlling trade between the Old and New worlds was highlighted by Philip's commission to build the Lonja (see **BUILDINGS 1**) in grand classical style.

Pilatos, Casa de: Seville's most sumptuous private *palacio* was completed in the early 16thC for the Marquis of Tarifa. The Marquis' decision to attempt a reconstruction of 'Pilate's House' resulted from a pilgrimage to Jerusalem in 1519. Instead of using Roman and Middle Eastern architecture, however, the house is an imaginative combination of Renaissance and traditional Andalusian *mudéjar* (see **A-Z**) styles and even some Gothic (see **A-Z**) details. The principal patio (see **A-Z**) with its intricate plasterwork and antique sculptures, and the grand staircase, richly decorated with *azulejos* (tiles) under a magnificent cupola, are particularly spectacular. The upper storey has frescoes and a series of rooms with paintings, tapestries and furniture. See **BUILDINGS 1**.

Plateresque: A 16thC architectural style peculiar to Spain. The term comes from *platero*, silversmith, and refers to the belief that the style's principal characteristic of rich and ornate decoration on the facades of buildings was derived from silversmithing. The decorative motifs came mainly from Italian Renaissance and classical Roman sources, although Gothic (see **A-Z**) elements were still often present, as in the Ayuntamiento (see **BUILDINGS 1**), Seville's best example of the style.

Police: The Policía Nacional wear a blue uniform and are mostly seen in urban areas, on foot or in white and tan vehicles. Report any crime to them and make a formal statement at their headquarters in Pl. Gavidia, tel: 4228840 (091 for emergencies). The Policía Municipal or Local (blue uniforms, white or blue cars), who deal mainly with urban traffic and enforcing municipal regulations, have their headquarters at Pabellón de Brasil, Paseo de las Delicias, tel: 4615450 (092 for emergencies). You'll see the Guardia Civil (green uniforms and caps) at immigration and customs posts and patrolling roads and rural areas. See **Crime & Theft**, **Emergency Numbers**.

Post Offices: Look for Correos. The central one is at Av de la Constitución 32 (parcels at Av Molini s/n). Mail to be collected must be addressed 'Lista de Correos'. Take your passport as identification for collections. A postcard is *una tarjeta postal*, a letter is *una carta*, a parcel is *un paquete*. All tobacconists (marked Tabacos) sell stamps. Postboxes (*buzones*) are yellow and may have separate slots, marked *extranjero*, for international destinations. See **Opening Times**.

Public Holidays: 1 Jan., 6 Jan., 19 Mar., 1 May, 24 June, 29 June, 25 July, 15 Aug. , 12 Oct., 1 Nov., 8 Dec., 25 and 26 Dec., and the variable holidays of Good Fri., Easter Mon. and Corpus Christi (see **A-Z**). Businesses and banks may also close or have limited opening hours during local fiestas.

Rabies: Still exists here as in other parts of the Continent. As a precaution, have all animal bites seen to by a doctor.

Railways: The central station, Estación Santa Justa, is on the corner of c/ José Laguillo and Av de Kansas City. There are daily services to Jerez, Cádiz, Huelva, Ayamonte (border with Portugal), Málaga, Córdoba,

Madrid, Extremadura, Gijón, Valencia and Barcelona. The 'Al-Andalus Express' is a luxury old-style train with modern facilities which does a four-day round trip from Seville calling at Córdoba, Granada, Málaga and Jerez. The office of RENFE, the national railway company, is at c/ Zaragoza 29, tel: 4414111.

Rejas: Decorative wrought-iron grilles are a distinctive feature of Andalusian buildings. In traditional houses they provide glimpses of interior patios (see **A-Z**), while in churches they screen special areas such as side chapels.

Religious Services: Your consulate (see **A-Z**) will be able to provide current information on places and times of worship.

Rocío, El: Andalucía's biggest and liveliest annual pilgrimage (*romería*) takes place in mid-May to El Rocío, a village in the sand dunes 65 km southwest of Seville, where an early wooden image of the Virgin was unearthed after the Reconquest. Pilgrims start out from Seville and other towns on Wed. or Thu. in horse-drawn wagons, on horseback or on foot. The highlight is the night of Sun.-Mon., when the image of the Virgin is carried in procession, but throughout the week there is much revelling. Traditional costume, known as *traje rociero*, is worn by many and the *sevillanas rocieras* (see **Sevillanas**) are sung and danced day and night.

Romans: In 206 BC, the Roman general, Scipio, defeated the Carthaginian army of Hasdrubal near Carmona and began building the town of Itálica (see **EXCURSION 1**). The area which forms today's Andalucía became part of the Roman province of Hispania Ulterior with its capital at Córdoba (see **EXCURSION 2**). In 45 BC Julius Caesar defeated his rival, Pompey, at the Battle of Munda and may have built walls around Seville, then known as Hispalis. The province was renamed Baetica, derived from Baetis, the Roman name for the Río Guadalquivir. However, by the beginning of the 5thC, the Romans' control of the region was under attack from a Germanic tribe known as the Vandals.

San Telmo, Palacio de: Av de Roma. Originally built as a nautical college, it was completed in the early 18thC. The elaborately decorated doorway, by the Figueroa family of architects, is an outstanding example of High Baroque (see **A-Z**). On the upper storey, a statue of San Telmo, patron saint of navigators, is flanked by those of San Fernando (see **A-Z**) and the Visigothic martyr San Hermenegildo (see **Visigoths**). In the 19thC the Palacio belonged to the Dukes of Montpensier, when its gardens extended as far as the Parque de María Luisa (see **WALK 4**). The interior is not open to the public.

Sculpture: Painted, carved wooden sculpture is peculiarly Spanish. Often very realistic and expressive, it can also be rather difficult to take at first for those used to the pure marbles and bronzes of the Italian Renaissance and classical Greece and Rome. Important masters included Pedro Millán, Martínez Montañés and Juan de Mesa, as well as the Roldán family of sculptors in Seville. Examples are in most churches and at the Museo de Bellas Artes (see **MUSEUMS**), and some are still used in religious processions such as Semana Santa (see **A-Z**, **Macarena**).

Seises: Ten choirboys in rich costume who perform 14thC dances with castanets in the Cathedral to celebrate Corpus Christi (see **A-Z**) and the Immaculate Conception of the Virgin (see **Events**). Originally there were only six, hence the name.

Semana Santa: Holy Week, from Palm Sun. to Easter Mon., is spectacularly observed in Seville. The processions of some 60 *cofradías* (brotherhoods) make an indelible impression on any viewer. Each *cofradía* has one or two *pasos*, floats of carved wood, which are borne by *costaleros*, strong men of the brotherhood or hired help. The revered images of the brotherhoods, most commonly a sorrowing Virgin, sumptuously dressed, rather than a figure of Christ, are displayed on the *pasos*, surrounded by flowers and candelabras. Sinisterly-hooded and bare-footed penitents, *nazarenos*, are part of each procession. Occasionally *saetas*, haunting laments of the Passion, are sung, originally by ordinary bystanders entranced by the images but now more commonly by strategically placed professional singers. The high point of intensity is from late Thu. night to Good Fri. morning: firstly, at midnight the procession of La Macarena (see **A-Z**) leaves her Basilica; at 0200 that of Jesús del Gran Poder leaves his chapel; from all around the city, other processions depart from their churches, winding different, tortuous routes through the city to the Cathedral to pass in front of the High Altar and returning home by another route. The city centre is closed to traffic during the *pasos*, and throughout the week most shops, banks, the Cathedral and museums have limited opening hours. Timetables of the *pasos* are given in the local papers.

Sevillanas: These dances of Seville, now so fashionable in all parts of Spain, began taking their present form in the mid-19thC. Originally they were courtship dances, in which partners danced very close but obeyed propriety by not touching each other. Each set of *sevillanas* is danced to a song consisting of four *coplas* or verses, during which the dance steps become progressively more complicated. Important qualities are soft, expressive arm movements (for women), perfect timing in interpreting the waltz-like rhythm and, above all, *gracia* (gracefulness and style). There are many variations, including the *sevillanas rocieras*, danced during the annual pilgrimage to El Rocío (see **Rocío**).

Sherry: *Vino Jerez*, Spain's best-known wine, is produced in the area centred on Jerez de la Frontera (see **EXCURSION 4**), Puerto de Santa María and Sanlúcar de Barrameda, southwest of Seville. The very chalky soil favours the grape types mainly used; Palomino, Pedro Ximénez and Moscatel. The wines are matured in bodegas by the *solera* system in which four barrels are laid one above another. New wine is added to the top barrel, mature wine is drawn from the bottom one and this ensures consistent taste and quality. A fino is very pale and dry; an amontillado is a fuller, older fino; an oloroso is more fragrant. Cream sherries are sweet; pale creams are less so. Manzanilla is like fino and only made in Sanlúcar. See **Drinks**, **Wine**.

Shopping: See CRAFTS, SHOPPING 1 & 2, **Best Buys**, **Markets**, **Opening Times**.

Siglo de Oro: Spain's Golden Age of the arts lasted from the latter part of the 16thC until the second half of the 17thC. Many of the contributors to this flowering of creativity were born or lived in Seville (see **Cervantes**, **Murillo**, **Valdés Leal**, **Velázquez**, **Zurbarán**). Other important names in Seville were: among painters, Francisco Pacheco and Francisco de Herrera (Elder and Younger), and among sculptors, Martínez Montañés, Juan de Mesa and Pedro Roldán (see **Sculpture**).

Smoking: Smoking is not allowed on city buses. Other places where smoking is not permitted include theatre auditoria, and there is also a ban in department stores such as El Corte Inglés. In general, however, smoking is still widely tolerated.

Sports: The best facilities are in clubs which have membership requirements. At Club Pineda, Av de Jerez s/n, tel: 4611400, the facilities include a 9-hole golf course. Club Antares, c/ Antonio Maura s/n, tel: 4621411, has modern facilities including a tennis and squash centre. The principal water-sports centre is Club Náutico de Sevilla, Av Tablada s/n, tel: 4454777. There are riding schools at Club Pineda and Hípica Puerta Príncipa, 11 km on the C 432, tel: 4860815. Enquiries about municipal facilities may be made at the municipal tourist office: there are comprehensive facilities, including a swimming pool, at Municipales Sevilla, c/ Ciudad Jardín 81.

Tapas: These are hot or cold snacks eaten as appetizers and usually accompanied by a drink. The simplest *tapas* are *aceitunas* (olives), for which Seville is famed. Other common ones include *tortilla* (omelette), *chorizo* and *salchichón* (smoked pork sausage), *jamón* (cured ham), *morcilla* (black pudding), *patatas en salsa del bravo* (potatoes in a rich sauce), *calamares* (squid), *salpicón* (seafood salad) and the ubiquitous *ensaladilla rusa* (Russian salad with tuna). Dishes of *tapas* are generally displayed on the counter and there is usually a list of prices. Be adventurous and you are likely to discover some delicious new tastes. Most bars serve *tapas* from about 1200, when Spaniards often have a snack, and again in the evenings. Larger portions are called *raciones*. See **TAPAS BARS**.

Tartessos: Some time before 1000 BC the state of Tartessos was founded in the Río Tinto area now covered by present-day Cádiz (see **EXCURSION 4**) and Huelva. It was known to the Phoenicians and the Greeks as the richest source of copper in the Mediterranean and was even mentioned in the Old Testament. The Carambolo Treasure in the Museo Arqueológico (see **MUSEUMS**) gives some hint of its fabulous wealth.

Taxis: Seville's 2300 taxis are inexpensive by international comparison. The first fare on the meter is 82ptas; a journey across the centre should cost less than 500ptas. Supplements include 52ptas after 2200 and 260ptas to or from the airport. Taxi ranks are found at major tourist sites, railway stations and near some hotels. Except at peak times, it is usually easy to hail a passing taxi. They are free when they show a green light on the roof and a *libre* sign in the windscreen. See **Tipping**.

Telephones & Telegrams: Hotels often charge heftily for communications services. The telephone area code is 95, and all Seville numbers are 7-digit beginning with 4. Cheap rate is 2200-0800.
Coin-operated booths require 5, 25 or 100ptas coins. Place coins in the sloping groove at the top of the coin box. Lift the receiver, check for the dial tone, then dial. Coins will drop into the box as needed. Codes for Spanish provinces and other countries are given in the booths. For local calls dial the number only. For international calls, after the dial tone, dial 07, wait for a second tone, then dial the country code and area code (exclude initial 0) number. At the Telefónica central office in Pl. Gavidia payment is easier (after the call) and assistance is available. Telex facilities are available at the main post office in Av de la Constitución and fax at the one in c/ Virgen de las Montanas, Los Remedios. For international telegrams, tel: 4226860 or visit a main post office.

Television & Radio: There are both public and private radio and television companies. Overseas services of some countries can be picked up on shortwave. The national television company (TVE) presents several channels in Spanish. Channel 2 features news in English, French and German 1230-1300 (June-Sep.). Many hotels offer satellite channels.

Time Difference: 1 hr ahead of GMT; 6-12 hr ahead of the USA.

Tipping: Although it may not be shown separately, a service charge is included on hotel and restaurant bills, but it's still the practice to leave around 5-10% in restaurants and to tip hotel staff for special services.

At the bar, leave a token tip, and 5-10% for table service. Taxi drivers, hairdressers and tour guides get around 10%, and lavatory attendants, doormen, shoeshines and car parking attendants 25, 50 or 100ptas.

Toilets: In c/ Fray Ceferino González, between the Cathedral and the Lonja (0645-2100 Mon.-Sat.). As public toilets are few, it is customary to use the facilities in bars without obligation to consume anything.

Torre del Oro: This 12-sided tower was completed in 1220 by the Almohades (see **A-Z**) as part of the city's defences. It was linked to a wall leading to the Alcázar and a chain stretched across the river to a similar tower on the west bank. The round top section was added in 1760 and houses the Museo Náutico (see **MUSEUMS**). See **BUILDINGS 1**.

Tourist Information: In the UK: Spanish National Tourist Office, 57 St. James's St, London SW1, tel: 071-4990901. In Seville: the municipal office is Oficina de Turismo del Ayuntamiento de Sevilla, Costurero de la Reina, Paseo de las Delicias, tel: 4234465, and it also has a kiosk at Pl. Nueva; the provincial tourist office is Patronato Provincial de Turismo de Sevilla, c/ Adolfo Rodríguez Jurado 2, tel: 4201091; the regional government, Junta de Andalucía, has a tourist information desk at San Pablo airport and a main office at Av de la Constitución 21, tel: 4221404.

Transport: As part of the huge development of the region for Expo '92 (see **A-Z**), new motorways have vastly improved access to the city. The new high-speed rail link reduces the journey from Madrid to less than 3 hr and passenger capacity at Seville, Jerez and Málaga airports has been greatly increased. See **Airport**, **Buses**, **Horse-drawn Carriages**, **Railways**, **Taxis**.

Traveller's Cheques: See **Money**.

Valdés Leal, Juan de (1622-90): One of the most important painters of the High Baroque (see **A-Z**) in Seville and, after Murillo (see **A-Z**), the most important Sevillian artist in the second half of the 17thC.

His best-known paintings are the macabre allegories of the vanity of worldly wealth at the Hospital de la Caridad (see **BUILDINGS 1**) but other paintings, such as at the Catedral (see **BUILDINGS 1**) and the Museo de Bellas Artes (see **MUSEUMS**), are more typical of his style, with dramatic perspectives, soaring figures and feathery brushwork.

Velázquez, Diego (1599-1660): One of the most famous of all Spanish painters and generally considered the greatest of the many important artists of Spain's Golden Age (see **Siglo de Oro**). He was born in Seville and was apprenticed to one of the leading painters of the time there, Francisco Pacheco, who became his father-in-law. By the 1620s he had moved to Madrid, where he became court painter to King Philip IV. Although best known for his work at Court, his early work in Seville, including some religious works, already showed his remarkable originality in compositions using daring perspective and in disarmingly direct and perceptive portraits. Few of his works remain in Seville but the Museo de Bellas Artes (see **MUSEUMS**) has some examples by him and his circle.

Venerables, Hospicio de los: It was completed in 1687 as a home for retired priests. Its church is notable for its works by 17thC Sevillian artists, including ceiling and wall frescoes by Valdés Leal (see **A-Z**) and his son Lucas Valdés. See **BUILDINGS 2**.

Visigoths: A Germanic, Christian people who were dominant in Spain from AD 475 until the Moorish (see **Moors**) invasion of 711. During the 6thC, there were factional struggles between followers of the Byzantine and the Roman Catholic forms of Christianity, during which San Hermenegildo, a Catholic, was executed in Seville by his father, King Leovigild. Catholicism became the official religion four years later in AD 589.

What's On: *El Giraldillo* is a free monthly listings publication, available at tourist offices and at some newspaper kiosks and hotels. Local daily newspapers such as *ABC* and the Andalusian edition of *El País* also give listings. See **Cita en Sevilla**, **Newspapers**.

Wine: *Vino* is *tinto* (red), *blanco* (white) or *rosado* (rosé). Spain produces some excellent wines in its *denominaciones de origen* (DOs), officially demarcated and controlled wine-producing regions, of which Rioja is the best known internationally, especially for its full-bodied, oaky reds. Many restaurants will have a *vino de la casa* (house wine). Regional restaurants will feature their own region's wines. *Vinos de terreno* are simple, inexpensive

wines from local bodegas, always best drunk young. Andalucía is best known for its *vinos generosos*, naturally high in alcohol and drunk as apéritifs or dessert wines. They are produced in its four DOs: Jerez (see **Sherry**); Montilla-Moriles, which produces its wines in a similar way and style to sherry; Málaga, which has delicious sweet red dessert wines; and Condado de Huelva, which produces sherry-type wine, *solera*, as well as white table wines. Before ordering a wine, see what local people are drinking and ask the waiter for advice. See **Drinks**.

Youth Hostels: The youth hostel, Albergue Juvenil, is at c/ Isaac Peral 16. For information on membership of the Spanish youth hostels association and advance booking, contact Red Española de Albergues Juveniles, c/ José Ortega y Gasset 71, Madrid 28006, tel: 91-5214427.

Zurbarán, Francisco de (1598-1664): After Velázquez (see **A-Z**) and Murillo (see **A-Z**), the third of the 'giants' of Spanish art of the 17thC, though still less well-known internationally than the other two. A native of Extremadura, the region west of Andalucía, most of his artistic life was spent in Seville. He became best known for his paintings for monastic orders, such as those for the Cartuja at Jerez, now in the Museum at Cádiz (see **EXCURSION 4**), though he was also a fine portraitist and still-life painter. His compositions are often strongly lit and startlingly direct.